The Wit & Wisdom
of the Founding Fathers

ALSO BY PAUL M. ZALL

Simple Cobbler of Aggawam in America

Comical Spirit of Seventy-Six

Ben Franklin Laughing

George Washington Laughing

Founding Mothers

*Becoming American: Young People
in the American Revolution*

Abe Lincoln Laughing

The Wit & Wisdom
of the Founding Fathers

BENJAMIN FRANKLIN

GEORGE WASHINGTON

JOHN ADAMS • THOMAS JEFFERSON

Selected and Edited by

Paul M. Zall

Introduction by

Roy Blount, Jr.

THE ECCO PRESS

THE ECCO PRESS • 100 WEST BROAD STREET
HOPEWELL, NEW JERSEY 08525

PUBLISHED SIMULTANEOUSLY IN CANADA BY
PENGUIN BOOKS CANADA LTD., ONTARIO

PRINTED IN THE UNITED STATES OF AMERICA

LIBRARY OF CONGRESS
CATALOGING-IN-PUBLICATION DATA

WIT & WISDOM OF THE FOUNDING FATHERS : BEN FRANKLIN,
GEORGE WASHINGTON, JOHN ADAMS, THOMAS JEFFERSON /
SELECTED & EDITED BY P.M. ZALL.—1ST ECCO ED.
P. CM.
INCLUDES BIBLIOGRAPHICAL REFERENCES (P.).
ISBN 0-88001-495-4
1. STATESMEN—UNITED STATES—QUOTATIONS. 2. FRANKLIN,
BENJAMIN,
1706–1790—QUOTATIONS. 3. WASHINGTON, GEORGE,
1732–1799—
QUOTATIONS. 4. ADAMS, JOHN, 1735–1826—QUOTATIONS. 5.
JEFFERSON,
THOMAS, 1743–1826—QUOTATIONS. 6. UNITED STATES—
POLITICS AND
GOVERNMENT—TO 1775—QUOTATIONS, MAXIMS, ETC. 7.
UNITED STATES—
POLITICS AND GOVERNMENT—1775–1783—QUOTATIONS,
MAXIMS, ETC.
8. UNITED STATES—POLITICS AND GOVERNMENT—1783–1809—
QUOTATIONS,
MAXIMS, ETC. 9. QUOTATIONS, AMERICAN. I. ZALL, PAUL M.
E302.5.W8 1996
973.4'099—DC20 96-16302

DESIGNED BY MARK ARGETSINGER

THE TEXT OF THIS BOOK IS SET IN ADOBE CASLON

9 8 7 6 5 4 3 2 1

FIRST EDITION

CONTENTS

❧

INTRODUCTION

BY

ROY BLOUNT, JR.

∽✣∾

IMAGINE THE pressure on a Founding Father. Generations to come will take whatever he says for What He Had in Mind. Original Intent. Over in England Dr. Johnson could write (*conceivably* with the colonists' lack of filial feeling toward their king somewhere in the back of his mind):

> If the man who turnips cries,
> Cry not when his father dies,
> 'Tis a proof that he had rather
> Have a turnip than his father.

What if even a hint of such sportiveness had found its way into the Constitution? Could anyone blame the sower-reapers of the Revolution for playing it straight? Cheek they had, but surely there was scant room, under the circumstances, for a tongue in it. Over in England William Blake was piping down the valleys wild. Americans had to put a nation together. Perhaps the British

{ IX }

notion that Americans have no irony, that we say exactly what we mean, derives from this period.

And yet we do—I believe—have irony, and always have. (Can I hear an *Amen?*) Here in this book we have the testimony of John Adams, of all people. In response to a Frenchwoman's assumption, on the basis of his last name, that he would be an appropriate person to ask about Adam and Eve's sex life (if there's anything the French lack it isn't irony). Adams rose to the challenge—after, he says, "composing my countenance into an Ironical Gravity."

I say "Adams, of all people." Before reading this book I would have said the same of George Washington. But in fact it appears that neither of our first two presidents lacked a sense of fun. Washington told tall tales. And when an Englishman complained that rebels shot at proper redcoats from behind walls, Washington wondered whether there weren't two sides to a wall.

Adams was pleased to recall the time he and Ben Franklin shared a bed in an inn, Franklin preferring the window open and Adams not. Before reading that anecdote, my assumption would have been that Franklin would have thought to himself, "Drat. I've got to sleep with Adams of all people. Oh well . . . this would've been a good one for the Almanac: Politics makes strange bedfellows." But Adams was no wet blanket. Abigail slept with him. We learn that in Tripoli—despite the risk that posterity would regard him as "a silly cur"—he established himself in his hosts' esteem as "a very Turk."

Franklin we know was droll. "Blessed is he that ex-pects Nothing, for he shall never be disappointed." (My mother used to say that, resignedly. I wonder whether she knew she was quoting such a gay old dog.) "There's a time to wink as well as to see." "The Horse thinks one thing, and he that saddles him another." But I'd always thought of him as the Fathers' designated wit. I never knew he was in good company. Nor did I realize that he could pull the British leg quite so Twainishly as to write, in a 1765 letter to the *London Public Advertiser,* "Whales, when they have a Mind to eat Cod, pursue them wherever they fly; and the grand Leap of the Whale in that Chace up the Fall of Niagara is esteemed by all who have seen it, as one of the finest Spectacles in Nature!"

No surprise that Thomas Jefferson could turn a phrase. "No more good must be attempted," observed author of the Declaration of Independence, "than the nation can bear." We will never hear that in a State of the Nation speech, but it's always there in the backbeat. "The way to silence religious disputes, is to take not no-tice of them," said Jefferson, who like Franklin and Washington was a deist, or freethinker, believing that God so loved the laws of nature that he refrained from meddling with them. Today we suffer the blather of politicians who profess to believe that His eye is on fed-eral regulations. What if sessions of Congress were opened with a moment of wit, instead of prayer? "Virtue and interest are inseparable," said Jefferson. If that prin-

ciple were stipulated by all parties, think what postur-
ing we would be spared. Jefferson also said, "Take things
always by their smooth handle." Has this book moved
me to retroactive chauvinism, or am I justified in finding something not just eighteenth century but also
distinctly homespun-American in the Founders' epi-
grams?

"Nothing dries sooner than a tear," said Franklin. As
well do most witticisms desiccate quickly. But not all of
them. Particularly ones that are dry enough, and suffi-
ciently wise to the laws of nature, to begin with. Hard
to imagine Franklin or Jefferson being quite so unicul-
tural as to come out with an effusion such as Henry
Fielding's, over in England. "All Nature wears a universal grin." Maybe Fielding was being ironic. Surely Dr.
Johnson (who would have made a great American, given
the opportunity) was not being baldly earnest when he
said in 1778, "I am willing to love all mankind, except an
American." Or maybe he lost his sense of humor for a
moment.

Maybe he envied revolutionaries who could maintain
a certain objectivity as they detached themselves from
subjection. The Catholic church has apologized to
Galileo, the Southern Baptist Convention to the civil
rights movement. I don't recall that England has ever
apologized for taxation without representation, not to
mention Valley Forge. Hey, that's okay. Never apolo-
gize, never explain, and all that. But the next time I hear
a Britisher aver that Americans have no irony, I will

think of Dr. Franklin's observation: "He that is conscious of a Stink in the Breeches is jealous of every Wrinkle in another's Nose."

If the folk that "Freedom" cries
Cry not as they crystallize,
'Tis a proof that they would druther
Have a Country than a Mother.

PREFACE

THIS BOOK came about because of my disappointment in such best sellers as Paul F. Boller's *Presidential Anecdotes* (New York: Oxford University Press, 1981) which take the Founding Fathers' words at second hand, and so miss much of the mirth at the birth of the nation. To show what I mean, this book offers excerpts from personal writings of our first three presidents along with a healthy sampling from Ben Franklin's writings for public consumption on the one hand, for friends and family on the other. The distinction points up my principle of selecting the presidential wit and wisdom from personal papers as opposed to their formal statements, and, more important, insofar as possible from original documents rather than secondary sources.

Ben Franklin, George Washington, John Adams, and Thomas Jefferson all grew up in the eighteenth century, an age with strict rules making your style fit your subject matter. A serious subject required high style, so nobody would expect to find Founding Fathers being funny in their official capacities, unless like Ben Franklin they were journalists grinding out propaganda with the grit of wit and wisdom. The same rules, however, encouraged slick repartee in conversation, and by extension in friendly correspondence, and that is why my excerpts come from letters, diaries, and overheard conversations.

My aim is not to humanize them so much as to open a window on their personalities otherwise obscured by our preconception of Founding Fathers as somehow supra human national monuments. This is not to devalue their achievements but to revise our own perceptions. Most still identify Franklin with his ventriloquist's dummy, Poor Richard Saunders, madcap almanac maker who filled his columns with nifty proverbs about thrift, industry, and delayed gratification that came to promote our acquisitive society. Early perhaps, Franklin himself practiced what Poor Richard preached but midway through life he mocked the wit and wisdom that enabled him to take early retirement at 42, so he could enjoy another 42 years in the courts, halls, and boudoirs of the western world. Yet it was the voice of Poor Richard that found the hearts and minds of the people at home and abroad. Not for nothing was John Paul Jones's ship named "Bonhomme Richard," the French for "Poor Richard."

Washington, too, saw the perils of public perception. In youth he suffered double indignity—for allegedly assassinating an unarmed diplomat and thus triggering the French and Indian War, and for rhapsodizing about the romance of battle in a letter intercepted by the enemy and circulated widely to make him the laughing stock on both sides. In the flush of age, by contrast, the world celebrated him for a double triumph—his victory over the mighty British war machine and his self-denying relinquishing his sword for plowshare. That self-denial was symptom of the self-control that stifled a natural affinity for wit and wordplay apparent in his revised private writings.

By judicious revision, Washington shaped the image of an awesome national monument which made him a hard act to follow for his successor, John Adams. Adams had neither the bearing nor the personality to take Washington's role. From youth he tried to acquire by nurture the shortcomings of his nature. Studying successful persons around him, he kept notes on the wise or witty sayings that appealed to audiences of different kinds. He treated funny stories with special care, including details about how they were told, in what dialects, and with what intonations. And when he repeated them, he would analyze his performance critically. On assuming the presidency which demanded higher seriousness, he did not follow Washington's practice of revising but instead completely rewrote even his autobiography to suppress the long-sought image of a more amiable John Adams familiar to friends and family.

Our own perception of Adams suffers, too, from comparison with his successor Jefferson, our most cerebral president. In a comment elevated to folklore, John F. Kennedy greeted Nobel-prize-winner guests in April 1962 as the greatest concentration of genius and talent in the White House since Thomas Jefferson dined alone. Jefferson's legendary brilliance was acquired through a process of "commonplacing," making succinct notes on everything he read—and that was voluminous—distilling its essence to fewest words. This habit became so ingrained in later life as to make him virtually unintelligible to casual audiences and so a target of popular satirists as an opaque metaphysician. But the habit also enabled him to reduce a world of wisdom down to wit worthy of Poor Richard's pages. This is especially evident in his letters to grandchildren or to most intimate friends, when he could sidestep the rules of decorum. In fact one of his enduring legacies is the best collection we have of Franklin's funny stories, some of which, I suspect, were of Jefferson's own devising, or at least revising.

Franklin, of course, had the advantage over the three presidents in that, as a professional writer, his role was that of an uncommon common man speaking to common men in their own middle-class language of conversation. Besides a higher class of language, the presidents had to put on the whole package of imperial ritual, adjusting monarchical trappings to leadership of a democratic republic. Constantly looking over one shoulder at jealous politicians in this country, they had to be concerned with appearances overseas, where a developing nation needed all the help we could get. Serious, sober demeanor may not have guaranteed a loan, but it did help to secure credibility in a world where decorum ruled.

—Paul M. Zall

The Wit & Wisdom
of the Founding Fathers

Benjamin Franklin

BEN FRANKLIN
LAUGHING

సౌకాౌ

L IKE ANY would-be gentleman of his era, Benjamin Franklin cultivated wit and humor to attain social grace but came to use the magical power of mirth as a way to help share wisdom with the people of an emerging nation. In the pose of madcap almanac-maker Poor Richard he showed them how to make a living, and later, as autobiographer, he showed them how to make that living worthwhile. Two hundred years after we became a nation, *Reader's Digest* credited Franklin "more than any other single person" with helping to shape the American character—which includes the ability to not take ourselves too seriously.[1]

His rise from homeless lad to world-class celebrity provided the model for countless generations. Adding to his story was the way he told it as an old man looking back on a youngster who was learning by doing, making mistakes while trying to get things right, and making up for those mistakes by helping others avoid them, all told with humor.[2] In this way, Franklin helped to encourage the American way of laughing at ourselves.

Given his recognized achievements, he could have

rested in deep conceit, and yet in his will he named his occupation simply as "Printer." He had gotten his start when a printer doubled as a writer and when the aim of a writer was to inform, persuade, and please. In that view a powerful sense of humor was a basic tool of the trade. And so it proved to be for Ben Franklin who, at age forty-two, was able to take early retirement and spend the next forty-two years doing whatever they couldn't stop him from doing in the legislatures, courts, and laboratories of the Western world.

In his day every printer needed to produce an almanac to stay in business. The common practice was to hire some mathematician to prepare the necessary tables and merely list other material. Franklin's *Poor Richard's Almanac* became a bestseller because of its comical prefaces and updated proverbs that filled the empty spaces in the tabulated columns, all in the voice of the madcap Richard Saunders.

As he described it, Franklin's own voice was entirely different: "In his common conversation, he seems to have no choice of words; he hesitates and blunders."[3] The botanist John Bartram, however, spoke of his "magical power of dispelling melancholy fumes" with his "facetious discourse."[4] And Franklin admitted that his "cheerfulness in conversation" made him popular.[5]

His letters, along with the occupational writing, reflect the same sort of cheerfulness in the loose style of conversation, peppered with anecdotes and proverbs as in the almanac. In an aside on lawyers, he claimed that in his country, they never buried lawyers when dead, but sat them down at the top of the stairs, and the next morning would find them missing—the devil having taken them.

Written down, stories such as these lose something. Considered as scripts for reading aloud, however, they open a window on Franklin's favorite way of getting laughs—the put-on. Not for nothing did the great realist Balzac call him the inventor of the put-on.[6] From age fifteen, when he started writing as the feisty widow Silence Dogood, he put on the pose of a series of humorous characters who would take on lives of their own—Anthony Afterwit, Alice Addertongue ("What else is gossip good for except to pass it on?"), Cecilia Shortface, and a legion of other comical creations.[7]

Sometimes Franklin's put-ons would be taken seriously. The most notable example of mistaken identity was Polly Baker, whose speech before a Connecticut court arguing that she should not be punished for bastardy was printed by historians as authentic till Franklin himself corrected the attribution. In our own time, some books still carry a mock advertisement with the British offering rewards for turning in scalps of American frontiersmen, including pro rated prices for those of men, women, and children, with no indication it was Franklin's satire on alleged atrocities.[8]

More often, however, the pieces were persuasive because they took a targeted argument to absurdity, as in letters to London newspapers urging that America send rattlesnakes to England in exchange for the British sending convicts here, or lamenting the threat to British economy from such American imports as sheep with tails so long they needed little carts trailing behind.

Of Franklin's many poses, however, none proved so persuasive, and at the same time informative and pleasing, as Poor Richard Saunders, who from the beginning of his almanac in 1733 admitted he was in the business to make enough money to stay in his wife's good graces. He peppered his pages with snappy sayings—"A countryman between two Lawyers is like a fish between two cats," witty and yet wise in advising against lawsuits. Despite all of Franklin's honors and degrees—Harvard, Yale, and Oxford—the world knew him best as Poor Richard.

The almanac made him a wealthy man. It sold ten thousand copies a year when the population of Philadelphia, then second in size only to London, was about fifteen thousand. Its success came from imitating two of London's most popular almanacs—the serious astronomical calculations of Richard Saunder (no *s*) and the madcap semi-astrological pages of *Poor Robin's Almanac,* for seventy years a staple of Englishmen's hearth and home. When Franklin's brother James printed an almanac in Newport, Rhode Island, he called it *Poor Robin's* in open imitation. Ben Franklin took it one step beyond, combining Saunder's instruction with Robin's pleasantry and mirth.

Poor Richard's Almanac was aimed at a class of people

who read little else. They depended on almanacs for information about time and tides, about when the moon would be full enough for them to travel at night, and sometimes about the weather. In time, Poor Richard also provided information similarly important to survival. In 1753, the public first learned how to protect against lightning in an article, "How to Make Houses Safe from Electricity," reflecting a shift in emphasis from entertainment to education, marked in the 1748 title, *Poor Richard Improved* after fifteen years of plain *Poor Richard.*

After twenty-five years, poor Poor Richard himself became the target of Franklin's fun. The Preface of 1758 told how Richard, waiting for the local bazaar to open, overhears secular preacher Father Abraham urging the crowd to practice thrift and industry by quoting not from the Bible but from *Poor Richard's Almanac*—"As Poor Richard says . . ." Spellbound, Richard is so persuaded by his own words that he postpones buying a suit of clothes to the next year.

Printed separately, Franklin's *The Way to Wealth* became one of America's bestselling books for a hundred years afterwards and the phrase "As Poor Richard says" proverbial. For more sophisticated readers, Franklin wrote comical satires for the newspapers and, while living in France, humorous pieces in French as a means of learning to write in that language. These, too, translated into English became staples of American schoolbooks and thus of mainstream culture.

Franklin's old age was miserably painful from gout, kidney stones, and prostatitis, yet he sustained the humor that had become second nature through habitual use in public and private life. He could be childlike in jesting for children, as in the epitaph for the deceased squirrel Skugg, household pet of English friends: "Here Skugg lies, Snug as a Bug, in a Rug." Or he could be brilliantly ironic, as in a newspaper piece purporting to be a letter from the Hessians' ruler complaining about loss of income from heavy casualties in America, a piece so subtle it took in some of Franklin's own friends. Rarely so savage as his model Jonathan Swift, he remained genial to the end.

He continued to revise his autobiography even to his deathbed, adding to the basic narrative started a decade earlier, interjecting little sketches or anecdotes to illustrate some point or expand an episode. But these were so consistent with his earlier pleasantry they could be identified easily in Franklin's manuscript as late additions.[9] Reminiscences of his friends reveal the same consistency in the sayings and fables heard in the Congress that passed the Declaration of Independence in 1776 and in the Convention that passed the Constitution a decade later.

Franklin would come to be credited even with bon mots expressed by someone else—as in the well known saying, "We must hang together or assuredly we shall all hang separately," more accurately attributable to Richard Penn. And later, tales about him would reappear as Abe Lincoln's—as in the one about Ben Franklin entering a country inn on a blistery winter's eve and asking the landlord to fetch a bushel of oysters for his horse; the curious loungers monopolizing the fireplace hasten to see a horse eat oysters, thus leaving the fireplace to Franklin. A later version substitutes Lincoln for Franklin and catfish for oysters![10]

One story about Franklin in his own time, probably apocryphal, tells about his presiding over the Pennsylvania legislature in his late seventies. It is said the legislators would humor him and his funny stories, waiting until he left to get down to serious business. More authentic are records of the Constitutional Convention that tell of an impasse in debate; when a fragile compromise came close to cracking, Franklin reminded everyone of the French girl who couldn't understand why, with so many people in the world, she was the only one who was always right.

Franklin's artful humor sustained a nice balance between persuasion, information, and humor. He could fool our contemporary historians into taking as authentic a mock list of prices offered by the British for the scalps of frontier settlers. Or fool them into taking at face value love letters written to Frenchwomen at a time when, in his mid-seventies, he was so incapacitated that the Queen lent him her litter to carry him to the harbor on his way back to America. He could fool everyone, but he remained true to himself as Benjamin Franklin, Printer.

NOTES FOR FRANKLIN INTRODUCTION

1. Bruce Bliven, "Ben Franklin," *Reader's Digest,* May 1976, p. 12.

2. P.M. Zall, "The Manuscript and Early Texts of Franklin's Autobiography," *Huntington Library Quarterly* 39 (1976) 381.

3. *The Autobiography of Benjamin Franklin,* edited by J.A. Leo Lemay and P.M. Zall (Knoxville: University of Tennessee Press, 1981), p. 39.

4. *Papers of Benjamin Franklin,* edited by Leonard W. Labaree, et al. (New Haven: Yale University Press, 1959–), 7:246.

5. *The Autobiography of Benjamin Franklin,* edited by J.A. Leo Lemay and P.M. Zall, p. 8.

6. See J.A. Leo Lemay, *Reappraising Benjamin Franklin* (Newark: University of Delaware Press, 1993), p. 412.

7. *The Pennsylvania Gazette,* 12 September 1732.

8. For example, *Laughter in the Wilderness,* edited by W. Howland Kenney (Kent, Ohio: Kent State University Press, 1976), p. 234.

9. *The Autobiography of Benjamin Franklin,* edited by J.A. Leo Lemay and P.M. Zall, p. xxxiii.

10. *Abe Lincoln Laughing,* edited by P.M. Zall (Knoxville: University of Tennessee Press, 1995), p. 42.

{ 1728 }

Epitaph written 1728.

The Body of
B Franklin Printer,
(Like the Cover of an old Book
Its Contents tore out
And stript of its Lettering & Gilding,)
Lies here, Food for Worms.

But the Work shall not be lost;
For it will, (as he believ'd) appear once more,
In a new and more elegant Edition
Revised and corrected,
By the Author.

—A parody composed as an exercise in the young men's club called The Junto, then circulated in manuscript among friends far and wide. His grave in Philadelphia bears only his name.

{ 1729 }

1. If we were as industrious to become Good, as to make ourselves Great, we should become really Great by being Good.

—From a "Busybody" column he wrote for the Philadelphia newspaper *American Weekly Mercury*. (18 February)

{ 1730 }

1. In a certain edition of the Bible, the Printer had, where David says "I am fearfully and wonderfully made," omitted the Letter *e* in the last Word, so that it was, "I am fearfully and wonderfully mad;" which occasion'd an ignorant Preacher, who took that Text, to harangue his Audience for half an hour on the Subject of "Spiritual Madness."

—From a "letter" in his own *Pennsylvania Gazette*, teasing about typographical errors. (13 March)

2. When the Company of Stationers in England had the Printing of the Bible in their Hands, the Word *not* was left out in the Seventh Commandment, and the whole Edition was printed off with, "Thou shalt commit Adultery," instead of, "Thou shalt not, etc."

—Ibid.

3. Through a whole Impression of Common-Prayer-Books, in the Funeral Service, where these Words are, "We shall all be changed in a moment, in the twinkling of an Eye, etc.," the Printer had omitted the *c* in "changed, and it read thus, "We shall all be hanged, etc."

—Ibid.

{ 1731 }

1. If all Printers were determin'd not to print any thing till they were sure it would offend no body, there would be very little printed.

—*Pennsylvania Gazette*, responding to complaints about his editorial policy. (10 June)

2. So many Men so many Minds.

—Ibid.

3. A certain well-meaning Man and his Son were travelling towards a Market Town with an Ass which they had to sell. The Road was bad; and the old Man therefore rid, but the Son went afoot. The first Passenger they met asked the Father if he was not ashamed to ride by himself and suffer the poor Lad to wade along

thro' the Mire; this induced him to take up his Son behind him: He had not travelled far when he met others, who said they were two unmerciful Lubbers to get both on the Back of that poor Ass, in such a deep Road. Upon this the old Man gets off and let his Son ride alone. The next they met called the Lad a graceless, rascally young Jackanapes, to ride in that Manner thro' the Dirt, while his aged Father trudged along on Foot; and they said the old Man was a Fool for suffering it. He then bid his Son come down and walk with him, and they travelled on leading the Ass by the Halter; till they met another Company, who called them a Couple of senseless Blockheads, for going both on Foot in such a dirty Way, when they had an empty Ass with them, which they might ride upon. The old Man could bear it no longer; "My Son," said he, "it grieves me much that we cannot please all these People: Let us throw the Ass over the next Bridge, and be no further troubled with him."

—Ibid.

4. Friday Night last, a certain Stonecutter was, it seems, in a fair way of dying the Death of a Nobleman; for being caught Napping with another Man's Wife, the injured Husband took the Advantage of his being fast asleep, and with a Knife began very diligently to cut off his Head. But the Instrument not being equal to the intended Operation, much Struggling prevented Success; and he was obliged to content himself for the present with bestowing on the Aggressor a sound Drubbing.

The Gap made in the Side of the Stonecutter's Neck, tho' deep, is not thought dangerous; but some People admire, that when the Person offended had so fair and suitable an Opportunity, it did not enter into his Head to turn Stonecutter himself.

—Ibid. (17 June), as local news.

{ 1732 }

1. In Bucks County, one Flash of lightning came so near a Lad, as, without hurting him, to melt the Pewter Button off the Wasteband of his Breeches. 'Tis well nothing else thereabouts, was made of Pewter.

—*Pennsylvania Gazette* (19 June)

2. Scandal, like other Virtues, is in part its own Reward, as it gives us the Satisfaction of making our selves appear better than others, or others no better than ourselves.

—Ibid. as "letter" from Alice Addertongue. (12 September).

{ 1733 }

1. He's a Fool that makes his Doctor his Heir.

—*Poor Richard's Almanac* (February)

2. Great Talkers, little Doers.

—Ibid. (April)

3. Eat to live, and not live to eat.

—Ibid. (May)

4. Fools make Feasts, and wise Men eat 'em.

—Ibid. (May)

5. He that lies down with Dogs shall rise up with Fleas.

—Ibid. (July)

{ 1734 }

1. An Ounce of Prevention is worth a Pound of Cure.

—*Pennsylvania Gazette,* in an article on preventing fires. (4 February)

2. Hope of Gain lessens Pain.

—*Poor Richard's* (April)

3. Neither a Fortress nor a Maidenhead will hold out long after they begin to parley.

—Ibid. (May)

4. Where there's Marriage without Love, there will be Love without Marriage.

—Ibid. (May)

5. Happy's the Wooing that's not long a doing.

—Ibid. (June)

6. Marry your Son where you will, but your Daughter where you can.

—Ibid. (November)

{ 1735 }

1. Early to bed and early to rise, makes a man healthy, wealthy, and wise.

—*Poor Richard's* (October)

2. A Lie stands on 1 leg, Truth on 2.

—Ibid. (July)

3. A Ship under sail and a big-bellied Woman, are the handsomest two things that can be seen common.

—Ibid. (June)

4. Nothing but Money is sweeter than Honey.

—Ibid. (June)

5. Keep thy Shop, and thy Shop will keep thee.

—Ibid. (June)

6. Three may keep a Secret, if two of them are dead.

—Ibid. (July)

{ 1736 }

1. Fish and Visitors stink in 3 Days.

—*Poor Richard's* (January)

2. He that lives upon Hope, dies farting.

—Ibid. (February)

3. Wealth is not his that has it, but his that enjoys it.

—Ibid. (March)

4. Let thy Maidservant be faithful, strong, and homely.

—Ibid. (April)

5. There's more old Drunkards than old Doctors.

—Ibid. (April)

6. She that paints her Face, thinks of her Tail.

—Ibid. (May)

7. God helps them that helps themselves.

—Ibid. (July)

8. The rotten Apple spoils his Companion.

—Ibid. (July)

9. The Absent are never without Fault, nor the Present without Excuse.

—Ibid. (July)

10. None preaches better than the Ant and she says nothing.

—Ibid. (July)

11. Don't throw Stones at your Neighbours', if your own Windows are glass.

—Ibid. (August)

12. Force shites upon Reason's Back.

—Ibid. (September)

13. Creditors have better Memories than Debtors.

—Ibid. (September)

14. He that speaks much is much mistaken.

—Ibid. (September)

15. He that scatters Thorns, let him not go barefoot.

—Ibid. (October)

16. Mary's Mouth costs her nothing, for she never opens it but at others' Expense.

—Ibid. (November)

17. God heals and the Doctor takes the Fee.

—Ibid. (November)

{ 1737 }

1. The worst Wheel of the Cart makes the most Noise.

—*Poor Richard's* (July)

2. A Countryman between two Lawyers is like a Fish between two cats.

—Ibid. (February)

3. The greatest Monarch on the proudest Throne is oblig'd to sit upon his own Arse.

—Ibid. (January)

{ 1738 }

1. The Scripture assures me, that at the last Day, we shall not be examin'd what we *thought*, but what we *did;* and our Recommendation will not be that we said, "Lord, Lord," but that we did Good to our Fellow Creatures. See Matth. 26.

—In a letter to his parents, who were anxious about his religious thinking. (13 April)

2. THE DRINKERS DICTIONARY.

A

He is Addled,
He's casting up his Accounts,
He's Afflicted,
He's in his Airs,

B

He's Biggy,
 Bewitch'd,
 Block and Block,
 Boozy,
Bowz'd,
Been at Barbadoes,
Piss'd in the Brook,
Drunk as a Wheel-Barrow,
Burdock'd,
Buskey,
Buzzey,
Has Stole a Manchet out of
 the Brewer's Basket,
His Head is full of Bees,

Has been in the Bibbing Plot,
Has drank more than he has
    bled,
He's Bungey,
    As Drunk as a Beggar,
He sees the Bears,
He's kiss'd black Betty,
He's had a Thump over the
    Head with Sampson's
    Jawbone,
He's Bridgey,

C

He's Cat,
    Cagrin'd,
    Capable,
    Cramp'd,
    Cherubimical,
    Cherry Merry,
    Wamble Crop'd,
    Crack'd,
    Concern'd,
    Half Way to Concord,
Has taken a Chirriping-Glass,
    Got Corns in his Head,
    A Cup too much,
    Coguy,
    Copey,
He's heat his Copper,
He's Crocus,
    Catch'd,
He cuts his Capers,
He's been in the Cellar,
He's in his Cups,

Non Compos,
Cock'd,
Curv'd,
Cut,
Chipper,
Chickery,
    Loaded his Cart,
He's been too free with the
    Creature,
Sir Richard has taken off his
    Considering Cap,
He's Chap-fallen,

D

He's Disguiz'd,
He's got a Dish,
    Kill'd his Dog,
    Took his Drops,
It is a Dark Day with him,
He's a Dead Man,
Has Dipp'd his Bill,
He's Dagg'd,
He's seen the Devil,

E

He's Prince Eugene,
    Enter'd,
    Wet both Eyes,
    Cock Ey'd,
    Got the Pole Evil,
    Got a brass Eye,
    Made an Example,
He's Eat a Toad & half for
    Breakfast.
    In his Element,

F

He's Fishey,
    Fox'd,
    Fuddled,
    Sore Footed,
    Frozen,
    Well in for't,
    Owes no Man a Farthing,
    Fears no Man,
    Crump Footed,
    Been to France,
    Flush'd,
    Froze his Mouth,
    Fetter'd,
    Been to a Funeral,
    His Flag is out,
    Fuzl'd,
    Spoke with his Friend,
    Been at an Indian Feast,

G

He's Glad,
    Groatable,
    Gold-headed,
    Glaiz'd,
    Generous,
    Booz'd the Gage,
    As Dizzy as a Goose,
    Been before George,
    Got the Gout,
    Had a Kick in the Guts,
    Been with Sir John Goa,
    Been at Geneva,
    Globular,
    Got the Glanders,

H

Half and Half,
Hardy,
Top Heavy,
Got by the Head,
Hiddey,
Got on his little Hat,
Hammerish,
Loose in the Hilts,
Knows not the way Home,
Got the Hornson,
Haunted with Evil Spirits,
Has Taken Hippocrates
    grand Elixir,

I and J

He's Intoxicated,
    Jolly,
    Jagg'd,
    Jambled,
    Going to Jerusalem,
    Jocular,
    Been to Jerico,
    Juicy,

K

He's a King,
    Clips the King's English,
    Seen the French King,
    The King is his Cousin,
    Got Kib'd Heels,
    Knapt,
    Het his Kettle,

L

He's in Liquor,
    Lordly,

He makes Indentures with
   his Leggs,
Well to Live,
Light,
Lappy,
Limber,

M

He sees two Moons,
   Merry,
   Middling,
   Moon-Ey'd,
   Muddled,
   Seen a Flock of Moons,
   Maudlin,
   Mountous,
   Muddy,
   Rais'd his Monuments,
   Mellow,

N

He's eat the Cocoa Nut,
   Nimptopsical,
   Got the Night Mare,

O

He's Oil'd,
   Eat Opium,
   Smelt of an Onion,
   Oxycrocium,
   Overset,

P

He drank till he gave up his
   Half-Penny,
   Pidgeon Ey'd,
   Pungey,
   Priddy,

As good conditioned as a
   Puppy,
Has scalt his Head Pan,
   Been among the Philistines,
   In his Prosperity,
He's been among the
   Philippians,
He's contending with Pharaoh,
   Wasted his Paunch,
He's Polite,
   Eat a Pudding Bagg,

Q

He's Quarrelsome,

R

He's Rocky,
   Raddled,
   Rich,
   Religious,
   Lost his Rudder,
   Ragged,
   Rais'd,
   Been too free with Sir
    Richard,
   Like a Rat in Trouble,

S

He's Stitch'd,
   Seafaring,
   In the Sudds,
   Strong,
   Been in the Sun,
   As Drunk as David's Sow,
   Swampt,
His Skin is full,
He's Steady,

He's Stiff,

He's burnt his Shoulder,

He's got his Top Gallant Sails
    out,

Seen the yellow Star,

As Stiff as a Ring-bolt,

Half Seas over,

His Shoe pinches him,

Staggerish,

It is Star-light with him,

He carries too much Sail,

Stew'd,

Stubb'd,

Soak'd,

Soft,

Been too free with Sir John
    Strawberry,

He's right before the Wind
    with all his Studding
    Sails out,

Has Sold his Senses,

T

He's Top'd,

Tongue-ty'd,

Tann'd,

Tipium Grove,

Double Tongu'd,

Topsy Turvey,

Tipsey,

Has Swallow'd a Tavern
    Token,

He's Thaw'd,

He's in a Trance,

He's Trammel'd,

V

He makes Virginia Fence,

Valiant,

Got the Indian Vapours,

W

The Malt is above the Water,

He's Wise,

He's Wet,

He's been to the Salt Water,

He's Water-soaken,

He's very Weary,

Out of the Way.

The Phrases in this Dictionary are not (like most of our Terms of Art) borrow'd from Foreign Languages, neither are they collected from the Writings of the Learned in our own, but gather'd wholly from the modern Tavern-Conversation of Tiplers. I do not doubt but that there are many more in use; and I was even tempted to add a new one my self under the Letter B, to wit, *Brutify'd:* But upon Consideration, I fear'd being guilty of Injustice to the Brute Creation, if I represented Drunkenness as a beastly Vice, since, 'tis well-known, that the Brutes are in general a very sober sort of People.

—The *Pennsylvania Gazette* (6 January)

3. Wish not so much to live long as to live well.
—*Poor Richard's* (August)

4. There are three faithful Friends, an old Wife, an old Dog, and ready Money.
—Ibid. (January)

5. Keep your Eyes wide open before Marriage, half shut afterwards.
—Ibid. (June)

6. If you wou'd not be forgotten As soon as you are dead and rotten, Either write things worth reading, Or do things worth the writing.
—Ibid. (May)

{ 1739 }

1. Blessed is he that expects Nothing, for he shall never be disappointed.
—*Poor Richard's* (May)

2. He that falls in love with himself will have no Rivals.
—Ibid. (May)

{ 1740 }

1. An empty Bag cannot stand upright.
—*Poor Richard's* (January)

2. Those who in Quarrels interpose must often wipe a bloody Nose.

—Ibid. (July)

{ 1741 }

1. He that teaches himself hath a Fool for his Master.

—*Poor Richard's* (January)

2. Ere you remark another's Sin, bid your own Conscience look within.

—Ibid. (April)

3. At 20 years of age the Will reigns; at 30 the Wit; at 40 the Judgment.

—Ibid. (June)

4. Wherever yet was ever found the Mother who'd change her Booby for another.

—Ibid. (June)

{ 1742 }

1. The close Mouth catches no Flies.

—*Poor Richard's* (February)

2. Late Children, early Orphans.

—Ibid. (March)

3. Death takes no Bribes.

—Ibid. (July)

4. To err is human, to repent divine, to persist devilish.

—Ibid. (November)

5. In my Travels I once saw a Sign call'd "The Two Men at Law"; one of them was painted on one Side, in a melancholy Posture, all in Rags, with this Scroll, "I have lost my Cause." The other was drawn capering for Joy, on the other Side, with these Words, "I have gain'd my Suit"; but he was stark naked.

—Ibid. (December)

{ 1743 }

1. The World is full of fools and faint hearts; and yet everyone has courage enough to bear the misfortunes, and wisdom enough to manage the Affairs of his neighbour.

—*Poor Richard's* (April)

2. The sleeping Fox catches no poultry.

—Ibid. (September)

3. If you'd have it done, Go: if not, send.

—Ibid. (November)

4. 'Tis easier to keep Holidays than Commandments.

—Ibid. (December)

{ 1744 }

1. Tart Words make no Friends: a spoonful of honey will catch more flies than Gallon of Vinegar.

—*Poor Richard's* (March)

2. Make haste slowly.

—Ibid. (April)

3. Sloth (like Rust) consumes faster than Labour wears: the used Key is always bright.

—Ibid. (July)

{ 1745 }

1. Wars bring scars.

—*Poor Richard's* (January)

2. Beware of little Expences, a small Leak will sink a great Ship.

—Ibid. (January)

3. A light purse is a heavy Curse.

—Ibid. (January)

4. Great Spenders are bad lenders.

—Ibid. (March)

5. No gains without pains.

—Ibid. (April)

6. In all your Amours you should prefer old Women to young ones. You call this a Paradox, and demand my Reasons. They are these:

1. Because as they have more Knowledge of the World and their Minds are better stor'd with Observations, their Conversation is more improving and more lastingly agreable.

2. Because when Women cease to be handsome, they study to be good. To maintain their Influence over Men, they supply the Dimunition of Beauty by an Augmentation of Utility. They learn to do 1000 Services small and great, and are the most tender and useful of All Friends when you are sick. Thus they continue amiable.

And hence there is hardly such a thing to be found as an old Woman who is not a good Woman.

3. Because there is no hazard of Children, which irregularly produc'd may be attended with much Inconvenience.

4. Because thro' more Experience, they are more prudent and discreet in conducting an Intrigue to prevent Suspicion. The Commerce with them is therefore safer with regard to theirs, if the Affair should happen to be known, considerate People might be rather inclin'd to excuse an old Woman who would kindly take care of a young Man, form his Manners by her good Counsels, and prevent his ruining his Health and Fortune among mercenary Prostitutes.

5. Because in every Animal that walks upright, the Deficiency of the Fluids that fill the Muscles appears first in the highest Part: The Face first grows lank and wrinkled; then the Neck; then the Breast and Arms; the lower Parts continuing to the last as plump as ever: So that covering all above with a Basket, and regarding only what is below the Girdle, it is impossible of two Women to know an old from a young one. And as in the dark all Cats are grey, the Pleasure of corporal Enjoyment with an old Woman is at least equal, and frequently superior, every Knack being by Practice capable of Improvement.

6. Because the Sin is less. The debauching a Virgin may be her Ruin, and make her Life unhappy.

7. Because the Compunction is less. The having made a young Girl miserable may give you frequent bit-

ter Reflections; none of which can attend the making an old Woman happy.

8th and lastly. They are so grateful!!

—In a letter Franklin passed off as genuine among friends. (25 June)

7. Many complain of their memory, few of their judgment.

—*Poor Richard's* (August)

8. 'Tis easier to prevent bad habits than to break them.

—Ibid. (October)

9. He that resolves to mend hereafter, resolves not to mend now.

—Ibid. (December)

{ 1746 }

1. When the Well's dry, we know the Worth of Water.

—*Poor Richard's* (January)

2. Good Sense is a Thing all need, few have, and none think they want.

—Ibid. (June)

3. The Tongue is ever turning to the aching Tooth.

—Ibid. (June)

{ 1747 }

1. There's a time to wink as well as to see.

—*Poor Richard's* (March)

2. A good Example is the best sermon.

—Ibid. (June)

3. What is serving God? 'Tis doing Good to Man.

—Ibid. (September)

4. What maintains one Vice would bring up two Children.

—Ibid. (September)

5. A Slip of the Foot you may soon recover: But a Slip of the Tongue you may never get over.

—Ibid. (October)

6. What signifies Patience, if you can't find it when you want it.

—Ibid. (October)

{ 1748 }

1. Remember that Time is Money.

—Opening of "Advice to a Young Tradesman, written by an old One," in a textbook for apprentices supposedly by George Fisher, pp. 375–77.

2. Lost Time is never found again.

—*Poor Richard's* (January)

{ 1749 }

1. Many Foxes grow grey, but few grow good.

—*Poor Richard's* (March)

2. If Passion drives, let Reason hold the reins.

—Ibid. (May)

3. If your head is wax, don't walk in the Sun.

—Ibid. (July)

4. All would live long, but none would be old.

—Ibid. (September)

{ 1750 }

1. Wouldst thou confound thine Enemy, be good thyself.

—*Poor Richard's* (March)

2. The rich Man who *must* die, was no more *worth* what he leaves, than the Debtor who *must* pay.

—In a letter to friend William Strahan talking about "dying worth a great sum." (2 June)

3. Little Strokes fell great Oaks.

—*Poor Richard's* (August)

4. Discontented Minds, and Fevers of the Body are not to be cured by changing Beds or Businesses.

—Ibid. (August)

5. Tim was so learned, that he could name a Horse in nine Languages; so ignorant, that he bought a Cow to ride on.

—Ibid. (November)

{ 1751 }

1. Pray don't burn my House to roast your Eggs.

—*Poor Richard's* (January)

2. He that is conscious of a Stink in his Breeches is jealous of every Wrinkle in another's Nose.

—Ibid. (March)

3. Don't judge of Men's Wealth or Piety by their Sunday Appearances.

—Ibid. (June)

{ 1752 }

1. For want of a Nail, the Shoe is lost; for want of a Shoe, the Horse is lost; for want of a Horse, the Rider is lost.

—*Poor Richard's* (February)

2. Old boys have their Playthings as well as young Ones; the Difference is only in the Price.

—Ibid. (August)

3. If Man could have Half his Wishes, he would double his Troubles.

—Ibid. (October)

{ 1753 }

1. 'Tis against some Men's Principle to pay Interest, and seems against other's Interest to pay the Principal.

—*Poor Richard's* (January)

2. God make man for Paradise, he make him for to live lazy; man make God angry, God turn him out of Paradise, and bid him work; man no love work; he want to go to Paradise again, he want to live lazy; so all mankind love lazy.

—In a letter to English friend Peter Collinson

quoting a Transylvanian visitor, Samuel Domien, who explained why primitive life appealed. (9 May)

3. The little value Indians set on what we prize so highly under the name of Learning appears from a pleasant passage that happened some years since at a Treaty between one of our Colonies and the Six Nations, when everything had been settled to the Satisfaction of both sides, and nothing remained but a mutual exchange of civilities, the English Commissioners told the Indians, they had in their Country a college for the instruction of Youth who were there taught various languages, Arts, and Sciences; that there was a particular foundation in favor of the Indians to defray the expense of the Education of their sons who should desire to take the Benefit of it. And now if the Indians would accept of the Offer, the English would take half a dozen of their brightest lads and bring them up in the Best manner. The Indians after consulting on the proposal replied that it was remembered some of their Youths had formerly been educated in that College, but it had been observed that for a long time after they returned to their Friends, they were absolutely good for nothing being neither acquainted with the true methods of killing deer, catching Beaver or surprizing an enemy. The Proposition however, they looked on as a mark of the kindness and good will of the English to the Indian Nations which merited a grateful return; and therefore if the English Gentlemen would send a dozen or two of their Children to Onondago the great Coun-

cil would take care of their Education, bring them up in really what was the best manner and make men of them.

—Ibid., explaining further.

4. Haste makes Waste.

—*Poor Richard's* (May)

5. He that is of Opinion Money will do every Thing, may well be suspected of doing every Thing for Money.

—Ibid. (July)

6. Anger is seldom without a Reason, but seldom with a good One.

—Ibid. (July)

7. If you have no Honey in your Pot, have some in your Mouth.

—Ibid. (October)

8. The discontented Man finds no easy Chair.

—Ibid. (December)

{ 1754 }

1. The Cat in Gloves catches no Mice.

—*Poor Richard's* (March)

2. The Horse thinks one thing, and he that saddles him another.

—Ibid. (April)

3. Love your Neighbour; yet don't pull down your Hedge.

—Ibid. (April)

4. The learned Fool writes his Nonsense in bet-

ter Language than the unlearned; but still 'tis Nonsense.

—Ibid. (July)

5. To be intimate with a foolish Friend, is like going to bed to a Razor.

—Ibid. (September)

{ 1755 }

1. You must practise *Addition* to your Husband's Estate, by Industry and Frugality; *Subtraction* of all unnecessary Expences; *Multiplication* (I would gladly have taught you that myself, but you thought it was time enough, and wouldn't learn) he will soon make you Mistress of it. As to *Division,* I say with Brother Paul, "Let there be no Divisions among ye."

—In a letter to 24-year-old Katy Ray, teasing her about an ardent lover by offering advice on how to behave after marrying him. (16 October)

2. An hundred Thieves cannot strip one naked Man, especially if his Skin's off.

—*Poor Richard's* (October)

3. Those who would give up essential Liberty to purchase a little Temporary Safety, deserve neither Liberty nor Safety.

—In an official reply to the Governor's complaint that the Pennsylvania legislature was not helping to defend the frontier. (11 November)

{ 1756 }

1. Love your Enemies, for they tell you your Faults.

—*Poor Richard's* (March)

2. As to our lodging, 'tis on deal feather beds, in warm blankets, and much more comfortable than when we lodged at our inn, the first night after we left home, for the woman being about to put very damp sheets on the bed we desired her to air them first. Half an hour afterwards, she told us the bed was ready, and the sheets well aired. I got into bed, but jumped out immediately, finding them as cold as death, and partly frozen. She had aired them indeed, but it was upon the hedge.

—To his wife, Deborah, reporting from a military mission on frontier. (25 January)

{ 1757 }

1. Nothing dries sooner than a Tear.
—*Poor Richard's* (January)

2. When they have long lived in a House, it becomes natural to them, they are almost as closely connected with it as the Tortoise with his Shell, they die if you tear them out of it. Old Folks and old Trees, if you remove them, 'tis ten to one that you kill them.

—In a letter to his sister Jane Mecom, arguing against moving their 78-year-old sister Elizabeth. (19 April)

3. One Today is worth two Tomorrows.
—*Poor Richard's* (April)

4. Work as if you were to live a hundred Years, Pray as if you were to die Tomorrow.
—Ibid. (May)

5. Dirt may stick to a Mud Wall, but not to polish'd Marble.

—Ibid. (September)

6. The Tongue offends, and the Ears get the Cuffing.

—Ibid. (November)

{ 1758 }

1. A Word to the Wise is enough.

—*Poor Richard's*

2. The first Mistake in publick Business, is the going into it.

—Ibid. (July)

3. Half the Truth is often a great Lie.

—Ibid. (July)

4. A full Belly makes a dull Brain: The Muses starve in a Cook's Shop.

—Ibid. (August)

5. Honey is sweet, but the Bee has a Sting.

—Ibid. (September)

6. We should restore it, that the French may, by means of their Indians, carry on (as they have done for these 100 years past even in times of peace between the two crowns) a constant scalping war against our colonies, and thereby stint their growth; for, otherwise, the children might in time be as tall as their mother.

—In a letter to the London *Chronicle,* offering reasons for giving Canada back to the French. (27 December)

{ 1762 }

1. I am going from the old World to the new; and I fancy I feel like those who are leaving this World for the next; Grief at the Parting; Fear of the Passage; Hope of the Future.

—In farewell to Scots friend Henry Home, Lord Kames, as Franklin concludes his mission to England for the Pennsylvania legislature. (17 August)

{ 1763 }

1. I am glad however that you have this Fault; for a Man without Faults is a hateful Creature, he puts all his Friends out of Countenance.

—In a goodhumored note to a longtime London friend, William Strahan, teasing him about not being as good-natured as he should be. (10 June)

{ 1765 }

1. The very tails of the American Sheep are so laden with Wool, that each has a Car or Waggon on four little Wheels to support and keep it from trailing on the Ground.

—In a letter to the editor of the London *Public Advertiser,* responding to complaints that American manufacturing undermines the British economy. (22 May)

2. Whales, when they have a Mind to eat Cod, pursue them wherever they fly; and the grand Leap of the Whale in that Chace up the Fall of Niagara is es-

teemed by all who have seen it, as one of the finest Spectacles in Nature!

—Ibid.

{ 1766 }

1. The whole Proceeding would put one in Mind of the Frenchman that used to accost English and other Strangers on the Pont-Neuf (a Bridge over the River Seine, leading to Paris) with many Compliments, and a red hot Iron in his Hand; "Pray Monsieur Anglois," says he, "Do me the Favour to let me have the Honour of thrusting this hot Iron into your Backside?" Zoons, what does the Fellow mean! Begone with your Iron, or I'll break your Head! "Nay, Monsieur," replies he, "if you do not chuse it, I do not insist upon it. But at least, you will in Justice have the Goodness to pay me something for the heating of my Iron."

—In *Pennsylvania Chronicle,* reprinted from the London *Public Advertiser* (March), protesting new taxes against the colonies. (23 March)

2. Two journeymen Snips, during the season of little business, agreed to make a trip to Paris, with each a fine laced waistcoat, in which they promised themselves the great pleasure of being received and treated as gentlemen. On the road from Calais at every inn, when they called for anything hastily, they were answered, *"Tout à l'heure, Tout à l'heure,"* which not a little surprised them. At length, "Damn these French scoundrels," says one, "how shrewd they are! I find it won't do—e'en let us go

back again to London." "Aye," says t'other, "they must certainly deal with the devil, or dressed as we are dressed, they could not possibly all at first sight have known us to be two tailors."

—In a letter to the editor of the London *Gazetteer*, countering Englishmen's complaint against New Yorkers' manners. (11 January)

3. As the proverb says, though one man may *lead* a horse to water, ten can't *make him drink*.

—As "Homespun" in the same newspaper, arguing against the tax on tea. (2 January)

4. I think the best way of doing good to the poor, is not making them easy *in* poverty, but leading or driving them *out* of it.

—As "Arator" in London *Chronicle*, arguing against government regulation of farm prices. (29 November)

{ 1768 }

1. Konnedohago, the young Warrior, took up the discourse, and said, "You tell us that the great Manitta made all things in the first six days. I find we know some things that you do not know. Your book does not tell you everything. At least if your Manitta made all the things of your country in the first six days, it was not so in the Indian country; for some things were not made till many generations after, and they were made by Manitta's Daughter. I will tell you," said he, "how it happened, as I learnt it when I last hunted among the Oneidas. Nine Oneida Warriors passing near a certain

hill, not far from the head of the Susquehanna, saw a most beautiful young woman descend naked from the clouds, and seated herself on the ground upon that hill. Then they said, 'This is the great Manitta's Daughter, let us go to her, welcome her into our country, and present her some of our venison.' They gave her a fawn's tongue broiled, which she eat and, thanking them, said, 'Come to this place again after twelve moons, and you will find, where I now sit, some things that you have never yet seen, and that will do you good.' So saying, she put her hands on the ground, arose, went up into the cloud, and left them. They came accordingly after twelve moons, and found growing, where she had pressed the ground with her right hand, corn; where with her left hand, beans; and where her back parts had pressed it, there grew tobacco." At this origin of tobacco, all the young Indians laughed; but old Canassatego, reproving them and the teller of the story, said, "You are a young man, or you would not have told before this white man such a story. It is a foolish Oneida tale. If you tell him such tales, what can you expect but to make him laugh at our Indian stories as much as you sometimes do at his?"

—In the same newspaper, a hoax review of a nonexistent book about Indian captivity. (28 June)

2. The situation in the colonies seems similar to that of the cows in the fable: forbidden to suckle their own calves, and daily drawn dry, yet they parted with their milk willingly; but when moreover a tax came to be demanded of them, and that too to be paid in grass

of which they had already too short a provision; it was no wonder they thought their masters unreasonable, and resolved for the future to suck one another.

—In the *Pennsylvania Chronicle,* on Parliament's tax policies. (12 December)

{ 1769 }

1. Mr. Grenville, speaking of the Inefficiency of the present Ministry, compared them to the two raw Sailors who were got up into the round Top, and understanding nothing of the Business, pretended however to be very busy. "What are you doing there, Jack?" says the Boatswain. "Nothing," says Jack. "And pray what are you about, Tom?" "I," says Tom, "am helping him."

—In a letter to Joseph Galloway, quoting opposition leader George Grenville's debate in Parliament. (7 February)

{ 1770 }

1. There is the Story of two little Boys in the Street; one was crying bitterly; the other came to him to ask what was the Matter? "I have been," says he, "for a pennyworth of Vinegar, and I have broke the Glass and spilt the Vinegar, and my Mother will whip me." "No, she won't whip you," says the other. "Indeed she will," says he. "What!" says the other, "have you then got ne'er a Grandmother?"

—In a letter to his wife, teasing her about spoiling their infant grandchild. (3 October)

{ 1771 }

1. In my first Voyage from Boston, being becalmed off Block Island, our People set about catching Cod and hawled up a great many. Hitherto I had stuck to my Resolution of not eating animal Food; and on this Occasion, I considered with my Master Tryon, the taking every Fish as a kind of unprovoked Murder, since none of them had or ever could do us any Injury that might justify the Slaughter.— All this seemed very reasonable. —But I had formerly been a great Lover of Fish, and when this came hot out of the Frying Pan, it smelt admirably well. I balanced some time between Principle and Inclination: till I recollected, that when the Fish were opened, I saw smaller Fish taken out of their Stomachs: Then, thought I, if you eat one another, I don't see why we mayn't eat you. So I dined upon Cod very heartily and continued to eat with other People, returning only now and then occasionally to a vegetable Diet. So convenient a thing it is to be a *reasonable Creature,* since it enables one to find or make a Reason for every thing one has a mind to do.

—From the first part of his autobiography, recollecting Franklin's break from Thomas Tryon's regimen of vegetarianism. (August)

{ 1772 }

1. 'Tis a most wicked Distemper, and often puts me in mind of the Saying of a Scotch Divine to some

of his Brethren who were complaining that their Flocks had of late been infected with *Arianism* and *Socinianism*. "Mine," says he, "is infected with a worse *ism* than either of those." "Pray, Brother, what can that be?" "It is, the Rheumat*ism!*"

—Sympathizing in a letter to Anthony Tissington about rheumatism. (28 January)

{ 1773 }

1. I had been some time with him in his Study, where he condescended to entertain me, a very Youth, with some pleasant and instructive Conversation. As I was taking my Leave he accompany'd me through a narrow Passage at which I did not enter, and which had a Beam across it lower than my Head. He continued Talking which occasioned me to keep my Face partly towards him as I retired, when he suddenly cried out, "Stoop! Stoop!" Not immediately understanding what he meant, I hit my Head hard against the Beam. He then added, "Let this be a Caution to you not always to hold your Head so high. Stoop, young Man, stoop—as you go through the World—and you'll miss many hard Thumps." This was a way of hammering Instruction into one's Head.

—In a letter to Samuel Mather recollecting his father, Cotton Mather. (7 July)

2. As a philosophess, she will not be discouraged by one or two Failures. Perhaps some Circumstance is omitted in the Recipe, which by a little more Experi-

ence she may discover. The foreign Gentleman, who had learnt in England to like boiled Plum pudding, and carried home a Recipe for making it, wondered to see it brought to his Table in the Form of a Soup. The Cook declared he had exactly followed the Recipe. And when that came to be examined, a small, but important Circumstance appeared to have been omitted. There was no mention of the Bag.

—In a letter to William Brownrigg, alluding to Mrs. Brownrigg's learning to make parmesan cheese. (7 November)

3. Though many can forgive Injuries, none ever forgave Contempt.

—In an ironic "Rules by Which a Great Empire May Be Reduced to a Small One" in the London *Public Advertiser.* (11 September)

{ 1776 }

1. Slaves rather weaken than strengthen the State, and there is therefore some difference between them and sheep; sheep will never make any insurrections.

—In Congress, debating the status of slavery.

2. The Doctor voted against it. Much surprize being manifested by some members, the Doctor in his justification, related an anecdote of the Celebrated Dr. Fothergill, who being desired by a Philosophical friend to say candidly whether he thought Physicians of real service to mankind, replied by observing that he must first know whether his friend included old women

among Physicians; If he did, he thought they were of great service.

—Debating the role of physicians in the new Army.

3. "We must be unanimous," observed Hancock on the occasion of signing the Declaration of Independence. "There must be no pulling different ways. We must all hang together." "Yes," added Franklin, "we must all hang together, or most assuredly we shall all hang separately."

—This celebrated saying was mistakenly attributed to Franklin by Jared Sparks in 1840.

{ 1777 }

1. Publicly he says that breaking the siege of the Congress is a blunder by General Howe, that it is not he who had taken Philadelphia, but Philadelphia who had taken him; that surrounded by enemy positions and with no free river for communication, he must either evacuate in turn or be Burgoynized.

—Reported in a Paris newsletter, *L'Espion Anglois*. (29 December)

{ 1778 }

1. I think it is Ariosto who says, that all things lost on earth are to be found in the Moon; on which somebody remarked, that there must be a great deal of good Advice on the Moon.

—In a reply to James Hutton, who asked his advice on making peace with Britain. (1 February)

2. A farmer, in our country, sent two of his servants to borrow [a harrow] of his neighbour, ordering them to bring it between them on their shoulders. When they came to look at it, one of them, who had much wit and cunning, said, "What could our master mean by sending only two men to bring this harrow? No two men upon earth are strong enough to carry it." "Poh!" said the other, who was vain of his strength, "what do you talk of two men? One may carry it. Help it upon my shoulders and see." As he proceeded with it, the wag kept exclaiming, "Zounds, how strong you are! I could not have thought it. Why, you are a Samson! There is not such another man in America. What amazing strength God has given you! But you will kill yourself! Pray put it down and rest a little, or let me bear part of the weight." "No, no," said he, being more encouraged by the compliments, than oppressed by the burden; "you shall see I can carry it quite home." And so he did.

—Comment on his appointment, as minister plenipotentiary to the French court. (14 September)

3. TO THE WORSHIPFUL ISAAC BICKERSTAFF, ESQ;
CENSOR-GENERAL
THE PETITION OF THE LETTER Z COMMONLY CALLED EZZARD,
ZED, OR IZARD, MOST HUMBLY SHEWETH,

He was always talking of his Family and of his being a Man of Fortune.

That your Petitioner is of as high extraction, and has as good an Estate as any other Letter of the Alphabet.

And complaining of his being treated, not with due Respect

That there is therefore no reason why he should be treated as he is with Disrespect and Indignity.

At the tail of the Commission, of Ministers

That he is not only plac'd at the Tail of the Alphabet, when he had as much Right as any other to be at the Head; but is, by the Injustice of his enemies totally excluded from the Word WISE, and his

He was not of the Commission for France, A Lee being preferr'd to him, which made him very angry; and the Character here given of S, is just what he in his Passion gave Lee.

Place injuriously filled by a little, hissing, crooked, serpentine, venemous Letter called s, when it must be evident to your Worship, and to all the World, that Double U, I, S, E do not spell or sound *Wize,* but *Wice.*

The most impatient Man alive

Your Petitioner therefore prays that the Alphabet may by your Censorial Authority be reformed, and that in Consideration of his *Long-Suffering & Patience* he may be placed at the Head of it; that S may be turned out of the Word Wise, and the Petitioner employ'd instead of him;

And your Petitioner (as in Duty bound) shall ever pray, &c.

Z

—Parody of legal petition satirizing Ralph Izard, an irritating fellow peace commissioner in Paris, Summer

1778, along with the "A Lee" (Arthur Lee) mentioned in Franklin's explanation in the left column. This purports to be from the Spectator Papers for his sister, Jane Mecom. (August)

4. When I was a Child of seven Years old, my Friends on a Holiday fill'd my little Pocket with Halfpence. I went directly to a Shop where they sold Toys for Children; and being charmed with the Sound of a Whistle that I met by the way, in the hands of another Boy, I voluntarily offered and gave all my Money for it. When I came home, whistling all over the House, much pleased with my Whistle, but disturbing all the Family, my Brothers, Sisters and Cousins, understanding the Bargain I had made, told me I had given four times as much for it as it was worth, put me in mind what good Things I might have bought with the rest of the Money, and laught at me so much for my Folly that I cried with Vexation; and the Reflection gave me more Chagrin than the Whistle gave me Pleasure. This however was afterwards of use to me, the Impression continuing on my Mind; so that often when I was tempted to buy some unnecessary thing, I said to myself, "Do not give too much for the Whistle"; and I saved my Money.

—In a *bagatelle*, one of his essays written as an exercise in French composition while living in suburban Passy, France. (10 November)

{ 1779 }

1. The Loss of friends is the Tax a Man pays for Living long himself. I find it a heavy one: for I pay it, not in depreciated Paper, but in Sterling Gold.

—In letter to New England friend Samuel Cooper from Passy. (27 October)

{ 1780 }

1. We make frequent and troublesome Changes without Amendment, and often for the worse. In my Youth, I was Passenger in a little Sloop, descending the River Delaware. There being no Wind, we were obliged, when the Ebb was spent, to cast anchor, and wait for the next. The Heat of the Sun on the Vessel was excessive, the Company Strangers to me, and not very agreeable. Near the river Side I saw what I took to be a pleasant green Meadow, in the middle of which was a large shady Tree, where it struck my Fancy I could sit and read (having a Book in my Pocket) and pass the time agreeably till the tide turned. I therefore prevailed with the Captain to put me ashore. Being landed, I found the greatest part of my Meadow was really a Marsh, in crossing which, to come at my Tree, I was up to my Knees in Mire; and I had not placed myself under its Shade five Minutes, before the Muskitoes in Swarms found me out, attacked my Legs, Hands, and Face, and made my Reading and my Rest impossible; so that I re-

turned to the Beach, and called for the Boat to come and take me aboard again, where I was obliged to bear the Heat I had strove to quit, and also the Laugh of the Company.

—In a note to Joseph Priestley counseling a mutual friend wishing to change his situation. (8 February)

2. He understood very little of French oratory, yet, wishing to be polite, he decided to applaud whenever he saw his friend, Madame de Bouffleurs, make any sign of satisfaction. After the meeting, his grandson exclaimed, "But, Papa, you were applauding whenever they praised you, and much louder than anyone else."

—A French friend, Abbé André Morellet, reports on Franklin at a banquet. (15 July)

3. I only mention as a Caution to you, never to go out of your Depth in Business, for the best Swimmer may be seized with a Cramp.

—In a letter counseling nephew Jonathan Williams. (27 December)

{ 1781 }

1. I have never known a peace made, even the most advantageous, that was not censured as inadequate, and the makers condemned as injudicious or corrupt. *"Blessed* are the peace-makers" is, I suppose, to be understood in the other world; for in this they are frequently *cursed.*

—In a letter to John Adams joining him on a commission to make peace with England. (12 October)

2. Receipt for a verdict in your favor: "Have reason on your side, procure an eloquent attorney to state it, an impartial judge to try it; and then, if you have great luck, you may gain your cause."

—From an interview with Priestley reminiscing about Franklin with the English writer Samuel Rogers and retelling his stories.

3. A man once came into the country . . . who asked, "What! do you bury lawyers? We place them in an armchair at the top of the stairs, and they are always gone before morning—the devil takes them."

—Ibid.

4. A Spanish judge satisfied everybody with his sentences. His son who succeeded him satisfied nobody. "What did you do, father? I read their cases with all possible care." "I did no such thing. I received their papers till each party was tired of sending them in. I then piled them in my pair of scales, and the heaviest scale had it."

—Ibid.

5. There was a sect at Philadelphia . . . which believed that a violent death was a sure passport to heaven, and many of them committed murder in order to be hanged. One of these enthusiasts set off into the fields early one morning with a determination to shoot the first man he met. It proved to be a Quaker, who saluted him so civilly that it disarmed him. He met nobody else; and, returning into the town, turned into a billiard-room where some persons were at play. There he stood

for some time resting on his gun. At last one of the play-
ers struck the ball into the pocket: "That was a good
aim," said his antagonist. "But this is better," said the
enthusiast, as he raised his gun and shot him dead. . . .
And what steps did the Government take? The sect was
very small, and it was thought better to hang them up
as they committed such crimes than to interfere publicly
to crush them.

—Ibid.

{ 1782 }

1. Men I find to be a Sort of Being very badly con-
structed, as they are generally more easily provoked than
reconciled, more disposed to do mischief to each other
than to make Reparation, much more easily deceived
than undeceived, and having more Pride and even
Pleasure in killing than in begetting one another; for
without a Blush they assemble in great armies at Noon
Day to destroy, and when they have killed as many as
they can, they exaggerate the Number to augment the
fancied Glory; but they creep into Corners or cover
themselves with the Darkness of night, when they mean
to beget, as being ashamed of a virtuous Action.

—In a letter to Priestly musing on man's inhu-
manity to man. (7 June)

2. A young Angel of Distinction being sent down
to this world on some Business, for the first time, had
an old courier-spirit assigned him as a Guide. They arrived over the Sea of Martinico, in the middle of the

long Day of obstinate Fight between the Fleets of Rodney and DeGrasse. When, through the Clouds of smoke, he saw the Fire of the Guns, the Decks covered with mangled Limbs, and Bodies dead or dying; the ships sinking, burning, or blown into the Air; and the quantity of Pain, Misery, and Destruction, the Crews yet alive were thus with so much Eagerness dealing round to one another; he turned angrily to his Guide and said, "You blundering Blockhead, you are ignorant of your Business. You undertook to conduct me to the Earth, and you have brought me into Hell!" "No, Sir," says the guide, "I have made no mistake. This is really the Earth, and these are Men. Devils never treat one another in this cruel manner. They have more Sense, and more of what Men (vainly) call 'Humanity.'"

—Ibid.

3. Avoid being concerned in the Pieces of Personal Abuse so scandalously common in our Newspapers that I am afraid to lend any of them here until I have examined and laid aside such as would disgrace us and subject us among Strangers to a Reflection like that used by a Gentleman in a Coffeehouse to two Quarrelers who, after a mutually free Use of the Words, "Rogue, Villain, Rascal, Scoundrel, etc." seemed as if they would refer their Dispute to him. "I know nothing of you, or your Affair," said he. "I only perceive that you know one another."

—In a letter to protege Francis Hopkinson, whose hobby was writing newspaper satires. (24 December)

{ 1783 }

1. There never was a good War, or a bad Peace.

—In a letter to British scientist Sir Joseph Banks looking forward to the end of the Revolutionary War. (27 July)

2. "These contests," he said, put him in mind of what had once passed between a little boy and little girl eating milk and bread out of the same bowl: "Brother," cried the little girl, "eat on your side, you get more than your share."

—James Madison recollecting Franklin's comments on Congressional conflicts and interstate rivalries.

{ 1784 }

1. Honor does not descend, but ascend.

—In letter to daughter Sally Bache, commenting on attempts to set up an American aristocracy based on the Cincinnati, officers in the Revolutionary War and descendants. (26 January)

2. I wish the Bald Eagle had not been chosen as the Representative of our Country; he is a Bird of bad moral Character; he does not get his living honestly; you may have seen him perched on some dead Tree, near the River where, too lazy to fish for himself, he watches the Labour of the Fishing-Hawk; and, when that diligent Bird has at length taken a Fish, and is bearing it to his Nest for the support of his Mate and young ones, the Bald Eagle pursues him, and takes it from him. With

all this Injustice he is never in good Case; but, like those among Men who live by Sharping and Robbing, he is generally poor, and often very lousy. Besides, he is a rank Coward; the little KingBird, not bigger than a Sparrow, attacks him boldly and drives him out of the District. He is therefore by no means a proper emblem for the brave and honest Cincinnati of America, who have driven all the *King*birds from our Country.

—Ibid.

3. In Truth, the Turkey is in comparison a much more respectable Bird, and withal a true original Native of America. Eagles have been found in all Countries, but the Turkey was peculiar to ours; the first of the Species seen in Europe being brought to France by the Jesuits from Canada, and served up at the Wedding Table of Charles the Ninth. He is, though, a little vain and silly, it is true, but not the worse emblem for that, a Bird of Courage, and would not hesitate to attack a Grenadier of the British Guards, who should presume to invade his Farm Yard with a *red* Coat on.

—Ibid.

4. You know every thing makes me recollect some Story. [A Gentleman] had built a very fine House, and thereby much impaired his Fortune. He had a Pride, however, in showing it to his Acquaintance. One of them, after viewing it all, remarked a Motto over the Door, "ŌIA VANITAS." "What," says he, "is the meaning of this ŌIA? It is a word I don't understand." "I'll tell you," said the Gentleman; "I had a mind to have the

Motto cut on a Piece of smooth Marble, but there was
not room for it between the Ornaments, to be put in
Characters large enough to be read. I therefore made
use of a Contraction anciently very common in Latin
Manuscripts, by which the *m*'s and *n*'s in Words are
omitted, and the Omission noted by a little Dash above,
which you may see there; so that the Word is *'omnia,*
OMNIA VANITAS.*" "O,"* says his Friend, "I now compre-
hend the Meaning of your motto, it relates to your
Edifice; and signifies, that, if you have abridged your
Omnia, you have, nevertheless, left your VANITAS legi-
ble at full length."

—Ibid.

5. You may see how people make shoes for feet
they have never measured.

—In a letter to Secretary of Congress Charles
Thomson, commenting on Frenchmen who submit
"wild and impracticable" plans for America. (14 June)

6. Do you not remember the Story you told me of
the Scotch sergeant, who met with a Party of Forty
American Soldiers, and, though alone, disarmed them
all, and brought them in Prisoners? A Story almost as
improbable as that of the Irishman, who pretended to
have alone taken and brought in Five of the enemy by
surrounding them.

—In a letter to William Strahan, on believing
British propaganda. (19 August)

7. They are pleased with the Observation of a
Negro, and frequently mention it, that Boccarorra

(meaning the Whiteman) make de Blackman workee, make de Horse workee, make de Ox workee, make ebery ting workee; only de Hog. He de Hog, no workee; he eat, he drink, he walk about, he go to sleep when he please, "he libb like a Gentleman."

—In the pamphlet "Information to Those Who Would Remove to America," describing the American people. (February)

8. A Man says something, which another tells him is a Lie. They fight; but, whichever is killed, the Point in dispute remains unsettled. To this purpose they have a pleasant little Story here. A Gentleman in a Coffeehouse desired another to sit farther from him. "Why so?" "Because, Sir, you stink." "That is an Affront, and you must fight me." "I will fight you if you insist upon it, but I do not see how that will mend the Matter. For if you kill me, I shall stink too; and if I kill you, you will stink, if possible, worse than you do at present."

—To a young writer, Thomas Percival, whose book condemned dueling. (17 July)

9. The Reverend, who projected [William and Mary] College, and was in England to solicit Benefactions and a Charter, relates, that the Queen, in the King's Absence, having ordered [Lord of the Treasury] Seymour to draw up the Charter, which was to be given, with 2000 pounds in Money, he opposed the Grant; saying that the Nation was engaged in an expensive War, that the Money was wanted for better purposes, and he did not see the least Occasion for a College in

Virginia. Blair represented to him, that its Intention was to educate and qualify young Men to be Ministers of the Gospel, much wanted there; and he begged Mr. Attorney would consider, that the People of Virginia had souls to be saved, as well as the People of England. "Souls!" says he, "damn your Souls. Make Tobacco!"

—In a letter counseling two young Americans then in England seeking ordination in the Anglican Church. (18 July)

{ 1785 }

1. They are angry with us and hate us, and speak all manner of evil of us; but we flourish notwithstanding. They put me in mind of a violent High Church Factor, resident sometime in Boston, when I was a Boy. He had bought upon Speculation a Connecticut Cargo of Onions, which he flattered himself might sell again to great Profit, but the Price fell, and they lay upon hand. He was heartily vexed with his Bargain, especially when he observed they began to *grow* in the Store he had filled with them. He showed them one Day to a Friend. "Here they are," says he, "and they are growing too! I damn 'em every day; but I think they are like the Presbyterians; the more I curse 'em, the more they grow."

—In letter to nephew Jonathan Williams, commenting on British rumors that America was heading for ruin. (19 May)

2. A Surgeon I met with here excused the Women of Paris, by saying, seriously, that they *could not* give

suck; *("Car," dit il, "elles n'ont point de tetons.")* He assured me it was a Fact, and bade me look at them and observe how flat they were on the Breast; "They have nothing more there," said he, "than I have upon the Back of my hand." I have since thought that there might be some Truth in his Observation, and that, possibly, Nature, finding they made no use of Bubbies, has left off giving them any.

—In a letter to London friend George Whatley, noting the increase in Paris's abandoned children. (23 May)

{ 1786 }

1. You need not be concerned in writing to me about your bad Spelling; for in my opinion as our Alphabet now Stands, the bad Spelling, or what is called so, is generally the best, as conforming to the Sound of the Letters and of the Words. To give you an Instance, a Gentleman receiving a Letter in which were these Words, "Not finding Brown at hom, I delivered your Meseg to his yf." The Gentleman finding it bad Spelling, and therefore not very intelligible, called his Lady to help him read it. Between them they picked out the meaning of all but the "yf," which they could not understand. The lady proposed calling her Chambermaid; "for Betty," says she, "has the best Knack at reading bad Spelling of anyone I know." Betty came, and was surprized that neither Sir nor Madam could tell what "yf" was; "Why," says she, "'yf' spells Wife, what else can it

spell?" And indeed it is a much better as well as shorter method of spelling "Wife," than by "Doubleyou, i ef e," which in reality spells "Doubleyifey."

—To his sister, Jane Mecom, after she lamented her bad spelling. (4 July)

2. Like the Man who in buying an Ax of a Smith my Neighbour, desired to have the whole of its Surface as bright as the Edge; the Smith consented to grind it bright for him if he would turn the Wheel. He turned while the Smith pressed the broad Face of the Ax hard and heavily on the Stone, which made the Turning of it very fatiguing. The Man came every now and then from the Wheel to see how the Work went on; and at length would take his Ax as it was without farther Grinding. "No," says the Smith, "Turn on, turn on; we shall have it bright by and by; as yet, 'tis only speckled. "Yes," says the Man; "but— I think I like a speckled Ax best."

—In the autobiography, part 2, talking about being content with "a faulty Character."

{ 1787 }

1. He spoke of the talkativeness of the French nation, and told a story of the Abbe Raynal—who was a great talker who came into a Company where a Frenchman talked so long and so incessantly that he could not get in a word—at last he cried out, "*Il e perdu—si il crache,*" "He is lost— if he spits."

—Benjamin Rush's notes on conversations with Franklin. (April)

2. The older I grow the more apt I am to doubt my own Judgment and to pay more Respect to the Judgment of others. Most Men indeed as well as most Sects in Religion, think themselves in Possession of all Truth, and that wherever others differ from them it is so far Error. Steele, a Protestant, in a Dedication tells the Pope, that the only Differences between our two Churches in their Opinions of the Certainty of their Doctrine, is the Romish Church is infallible, and the Church of England is never in the Wrong.

—Addressing the Constitutional Convention's closing session. (17 September)

3. But though many private Persons think almost as highly of their own Infallibility, as that of their Sect, few express it so naturally as a certain French lady, who in a little Dispute with her Sister, said, "I don't know how it happens, Sister, but I meet with nobody but myself that's always in the right."

—Ibid.

4. Whilst the last members were signing, Doctor Franklin looking towards the President's Chair, at the back of which a rising sun happened to be painted, observed to a few members near him, that Painters had found it difficult to distinguish in their art a rising from a setting sun. . . . "But now at length I have the happiness to know it is a rising and not a setting Sun."

—James Madison recording the final session of the Convention.

5. When the sessions were over, a lady asked Franklin: "Well, Doctor, what have we got, a republic or a monarchy?" "A republic," replied the doctor, "if you can keep it."

—Historian Max Farrand reporting on the same event.

{ 1788 }

1. A narrator was relating a dispute that happened between Queen Anne and the Archbishop of Canterbury, concerning a vacant mitre, which the Queen was for bestowing on a person the Archbishop thought unworthy, made both the Queen and the Archbishop swear three or four thumping oaths in every sentence of the discussion, and the Archbishop at last gained his point. One present at this tale, being surprised, said, "But did the Queen and the Archbishop swear so at one another?" "O no, no," says the relator; "that is only my way of telling the story."

—In letter to sister Jane Mecom explaining why the press misrepresented his 1767 story about the hot poker. (26 November)

{ 1789 }

1. Our new Constitution is now established, and has an appearance that promises permanency; but in

this world nothing can be said to be certain, except death and taxes.

—In letter to French friend Jean-Baptiste LeRoy. (13 November)

{ 1790 }

1. The Doctor remarked that he should be glad to see an experiment made of a religion that admitted no pardon for transgressions; the hope of impunity being the great encouragement to them. In illustration of this tendency, he said that when he was a young man he was much subject to fits of indigestion brought on by indulgence at the table. On complaining of it to a friend, he recommended as a remedy a few drops of wormwood whenever that happened; and that he should carry a little vial of it about him. On trial he found the remedy to answer. "And then," said he, "having my absolution in my pocket, I went on sinning more freely than ever."

—In James Madison's memorandum of visiting Franklin on his sick bed. (January)

2. A few days before he died, he rose from his bed and begged that it might be made up for him so that he might die "in a decent manner." His daughter told him that she hoped he would recover and live many years longer. He calmly replied he "hoped not." Upon being advised to change his position in bed that he might breathe "easy," he said, "A dying man can do nothing easy."

—Benjamin Rush reports to Richard Price on Franklin's death on 17 April. (24 April)

George Washington

GEORGE WASHINGTON
LAUGHING

༄༅༎

ABANDONING George the Third, Americans needed someone else to revere and so devised the icon of George Washington. He helped develop the demigod image by playing the role expected of him even if it meant wrenching his personality to fit the part. He had to overcome a natural shyness often mistaken for arrogance and control a nasty temper along with a biting sense of humor, magisterial yet given to low puns—as when appealing to Congress for troops' pay and was told the treasurer had his hands full, Washington riposted, "He wished he had his pockets full, too."

Thanks to his lifelong practice of keeping notes and correspondence, and never throwing anything away, he left plenty of clues as to the real George Washington. Some visitors were often taken aback by his ready wit. When Mrs. Washington chided him for saying grace even though a clergyman present should have had that honor, Washington excused himself by explaining that he did not wish the clergyman to think this household was entirely "graceless."

Visitors could be more taken in by tall tales that were

out of keeping with his austere reputation. He assured one British visitor that mosquitoes near Lake Champlain could bite through thick army boots and a visitor from Boston that Mount Vernon toads' stomachs lit up at night from eating fireflies. Such nonsense would be passed on with the sobriety everyone expected of him.

Some of his wit can have a tone of sarcasm. When Alexander Hamilton came in late for a meeting, Washington muttered, "You must provide yourself with a new watch—or I a new secretary." Or, when the French radical Volney asked for a letter of introduction in this country, Washington wrote out: "C. Volney needs no introduction from Geo. Washington." Even in the privacy of docketing his mail, Washington could be witty: Thomas Bruff, a total stranger, claimed he had a vision which required 500 pounds to be fulfilled. Washington recorded the request: "From Thomas Bruff—without date and without Success."

His diary, too, reveals the same kind of self-amusement: A Sunday entry made from York, Pennsylvania, records that the locals had no Episcopal church and so he had attended the Dutch Reformed church, hastening to reassure the diary that there should be no anxiety about his being converted, since the sermon had been entirely in German, and he'd understood not one word.

Apart from his private life, Washington's public image was being cloaked with idolatry. Within a year after John Adams nominated him to be commander-in-chief, Adams himself warned Congress about idolizing "an image which our own hands" created.[1] Before war's end, the press were haling him as "the Saviour of his Country."[2] By the time of the Constitutional Convention in 1787, his appearance alone evoked awe usually reserved for gods.

When someone in Convention Hall dropped a copy of the secret drafts of convention proceedings, Washington retrieved the paper. He kept it in his pocket till adjournment, then said: "I am sorry to find that some one Member of this Body has been so neglectful of the secrets of the Convention as to drop a copy of their proceedings. I must entreat Gentlemen to be more careful lest our transactions get into the News Papers and disturb the public repose by premature speculations."[3] Then came a voice of doom as he closed: "I know not whose Paper it is, but there it is (throwing it down on the table), let him who owns it take it." Nobody did.

In devising the office of president under the new Constitution, the delegates endowed the office with more powers than they would have given it had they not had the model before them. He spoke in the debates only once, urging compromise at the end, but his influence was felt both inside and outside the Hall. Crowds followed him on rare holidays, even on a nostalgic visit to Valley Forge and on a fishing trip.

As he ascended his new office, Washington was faced with reconciling the rhetoric of democracy and the ritual of monarchy. Congress debated hard on what to call him, considering "Your excellency" and "Your highness" before settling on "Mr. President." Washington tread very carefully: "There is scarcely any part of my conduct which may not hereafter be drawn into precedent."[4] Three times he rejected the Mint's proposal to engrave coins with his likeness on them.

Madison noted that, while not "idolizing public opinion, no man could be more attentive to the means for ascertaining it."[5] Through private correspondence, polling his friends, and reading newspapers, he kept his finger on the public pulse. Even critical observers were soon impressed by his imperial bearing. They bandied about words to describe his aura of natural dignity: "cold, reserved, even phlegmatic, though without the least appearance of haughtiness or ill-nature."[6]

The other side of that coin was an increase in public criticism of his administration. Jefferson saw Washington's reaction: "By god, he had rather be in his grave than in his present situation. That he had rather be on his farm than to be made emperor of the world and yet they were charging him with wanting to be a king."[7] He increasingly looked upon attacks on the presidency as attacks on his integrity aimed at eroding public confidence in the office and finally in the American form of government itself.

In refusing to serve a third term, he asked Alexander Hamilton to revise his farewell address, which was drafted in heat. He wished it to appear in "an honest, unaffected simple garb," with "egotisms—however just they may be" removed.[8] He also asked Hamilton to cut out pointed allusions and "expressions which could not fail to draw upon me attacks which I should wish to avoid." Hamilton subsequently transformed a self-pitying complaint into a dignified, statesmanlike assessment of Washington's basic principles and policy.

Washington asked friends also to look over official correspondence "with as critical an eye"[9] as the opposition press would employ, hoping thereby to anticipate and blunt criticism which, indeed, grew particularly vicious after he announced retirement. Philadelphia editor William Duane editorialized about the farewell address as "the loathings of a sick mind."[10] The Philadelphia *Aurora* reached a new low in asserting: "If ever a nation was debauched by a man, the American Nation has been debauched by Washington."[11]

The opposition claimed their attacks were justified "to expose the PERSONAL IDOLATRY into which we have been needlessly running."[12] In retiring, Washington did his best to seek a low profile. At the inauguration of successor John Adams, he wore a conservative, dark suit, stood aside and insisted that the new president precede him to the ceremonies. But an entire generation had grown up under his benevolent gaze. A basic book on child development advised parents: "Begin with the infant in his cradle; let the first word he lisps be the name of WASHINGTON."[13]

Mount Vernon had become a national shrine, especially for visitors from abroad. One Russian noted:

"Every American considers it his sacred duty to have Washington's likeness in his home, just as we have images of God's saints." The canonization was complete and would remain irreversible for centuries.

On Washington's death, more than 400 tracts and pamphlets eulogized his suprahuman achievements. The *Monthly Magazine* almost alone reminded Americans that the public figure they knew also had a more human side, had "perfectly relished a sally of wit or a pleasant story."[14] Bishop White then recollected that the former president's last supper had been marked by gaiety and laughter. These light-hearted recollections were not intended to humanize Washington but merely stated facts successfully submerged by his friends along with a little help from himself.

Shortly after the war, Washington had hired a staff to organize his official correspondence and took the opportunity to revise his private correspondence in order to bring earlier writings into line with his later standing as world-class hero.[15] This was increasingly important when, as president, he sought to establish the nation as worthy of serious recognition abroad. The result of this cleansing was the submergence of Washington's comic spirit in both public and private records.

An early letter to his brother Jack predates Mark Twain's classic statement about reports of his death having been grossly exaggerated. One of his last letters teased a friend, then Secretary of War, about press reports of corruption in the administration, especially a rumored $800,000 bribe: "Pray, good sir, what part of the $800,000 have come to your share? As you are high in Office, I hope you did not disgrace yourself in the acceptance of a paltry bribe—$100,000 perhaps."

This kind of humor soon disappeared from public view as his own pruning was supplemented by later historians zealous to protect his sanctity even at the cost of common sense. The first official editor of Washington's papers, Jared Sparks, deleted such "low" expressions as the description of a sum of money as "but a flea-bite," which Sparks rewrote: "totally inadequate."[16] He doggedly omitted similar expressions: "General Fry at present keeps his room, and talks learnedly of emetics and cathartics."[17]

The worst case of editing, however, came in the mid-1920s. Banker J.P. Morgan had collected Washington papers for years, but his personal librarian confessed to destroying those whose earthy language would have undermined the icon worshipped by American youth.[18] Luckily, Washington had acquired the habit of making and keeping copies of letters, especially during wartime when they could have been captured en route. Some documents exist in multiple copies—an original, a draft sent to the addressee, a duplicate in case of intervention, a clerk's copy for filing, and an official copy made by a government agent.[19] Studying the copies shows Washington sometimes revised the same document as long as he lived.

Given these opportunities for revising the public

record, it should suprise nobody that so little whimsy survived those years when Washington's position required a perception of high moral seriousness. The University of Virginia's mammoth project of publishing all versions of Washington's writings should go far to restoring our view of the real Washington. Meanwhile perennial polls show that he no longer reigns first in the hearts of his countrymen. In the twentieth century he has been supplanted by the more amiable Abe Lincoln. Perhaps the reason lies in Lincoln's having been assassinated "to make us free," while Washington lived on only to die from medical bloodletting in his own bed. Whatever the cause, the irony remains that Lincoln, naturally melancholy, carefully cultivated popular humor in the national interest[20] while Washington, naturally witty, suppressed his sense of humor for the same sake.

NOTES TO WASHINGTON INTRODUCTION

1. *Letters of Delegates to Congress,* ed. Paul Smith (Washington: Library of Congress, 1975–), 6:323–25.

2. *Pennsylvania Gazette* 21 November 1781; *Freeman's Journal* 4 December 1781.

3. "William Pierce, on the Federal Convention of 1787," *American Historical Review* 3 (1898):324–25, collated with manuscript in Connecticut State Library, 342.732/P611c.

4. *Writings of Washington,* ed. J.C. Fitzpatrick (Washington: Government Printing Office, 1932–40), 30:496.

5. James Madison, "Detached Memoranda," *William & Mary Quarterly* 3d ser., 3(1946):541.

6. *Selections from the Letters and Correspondence of Sir James Bland Burges,* ed. James Hutton (London: John Murray, 1885), 201.

7. "Anas" 2 August 1793, *Writings,* ed. Paul Leicester Ford, 1:254.

8. *Washington's Farewell Address,* ed. Victor Hugo Paltsits (New York: New York Public Library, 1935), 241–42.

9. *Writings of Washington* 35:144–45.

10. *A Letter to George Washington* (Philadelphia, 1796), 26.

11. Donald H. Stewart, *The Opposition Press* (Albany: State University of New York Press, 1969), 533.

12. "Jasper Dwight," *A Letter to George Washington,* 48.

13. Noah Webster, *An American Selection of Lessons in Reading and Speaking* (Philadelphia: Young & M'Culloch, 1787), epigraph.

14. Bird Wilson, *Memoir of the Life of William White* (Philadelphia: Kay, 1839), 191–92.

15. John D. Knowlton, "Properly Arranged and so Correctly Recorded," *American Archivist* 27 (1964):371–74.

16. *Original Letters from Washington to Joseph Reed,* ed. W.B. Reed (Philadelphia: A. Hart, 1852) gives examples in parallel columns; *Letter to Jared Sparks by Lord Mahon* (London: John Murray, 1852), 9.

17. *Lord Mahon,* 26.

18. Edward Laroque Tinker, "Whitewashing," *The Bookman* 60 (February 1925):719.

19. "Properly Arranged," 371–74.

20. *Abe Lincoln Laughing,* ed. P.M. Zall (Knoxville: University of Tennessee Press, 1995), 42.

{ 1755 }

1. As I have heard since my arrival at this place a circumstantial account of my death and dying Speech; I take this early oppertunity of contradicting the *first,* and of assuring you, that I have not, as yet, composed the *latter.*

—In a letter to his brother, Jack, from the frontier reassuring him that reports of Washington's death had been exaggerated. (18 July)

{ 1760 }

1. One being lost on the way—as the others might as well have been for their goodness.

—Notebook entry on hogs bought from David French. (8 January)

2. Colonel Cocke was disgusted at my House, and left because he see an old Negroe there resembling his own Image.

—Notebook entry. (12 January)

{ 1762 }

1. I am told you have lately introduced into your Family, a certain production which you are lost in admiration of, and spend so much time in contemplating the just proportion of its parts, the ease, and conveniences with which it abounds, that it is thought you will have little time to animadvert upon the prospect of your crops etc.; pray how will this be reconciled to that anxious care and vigilance, which is so escencially necessary at a time when our growing Prosperity, meaning the Tobacco, is assailed by every villainous worm that has had an existence since the days of Noah (how unkind it was of Noah now I have mentioned his name to suffer such a brood of vermin to get a birth in the Ark) but perhaps you may be as well off as we are; that is, have no To-

bacco for them to eat and there I think we nicked the Dogs.

—In a letter to brother-in-law Burwell Bassett on the birth of a baby. (28 August)

{ 1773 }

1. Mentioning of one wedding puts me in mind of another, though of less dignity; this is the marriage of Mr. Henderson (of Colchester) to a Miss More (of the same place) remarkable for a very frizzled head, and good singing, the latter of which I shall presume it was that captivated our merchant.

—In a letter to Bassett, reporting local gossip. (15 February)

{ 1776 }

1. Colonel Paterson assured him that they had the highest personal respect for General Washington, and did not mean to derogate from his rank; that the letter, of which he was now the bearer from the Commissioners, was directed to George Washington, Esq., etc. etc. etc. which they hoped would remove all difficulties; as the three "et ceteras" might be understood to imply everything that ought to follow. To this the General replied, that though it was true the three "et ceteras" might mean "everything," it was also true they might mean "anything."

—James Thacher's military journal reports this exchange with British Colonel James Paterson, who tried to deliver a letter addressed to Mr. rather than General Washington. (20 July)

{ 1779 }

1. Since our arrival at this happy spot, we have had a Ham (sometimes a shoulder) of Bacon to grace the head of the table; a piece of roast Beef adorns the foot; and a small dish of Greens or Beans (almost imperceptible) decorates the center. When the Cook has a mind to cut a figure (and this I presume he will attempt to do tomorrow) we have two Beefstake-Pyes, or dishes of Crabs in addition, one on each side the center dish, dividing the space, and reducing the distance between dish and dish to about Six feet, which without them, would be near twelve apart. Of late he has had the surprizing segacity to discover, that apples will make pyes; and it's a question if, amidst the violence of his efforts, we do not get one of the apples instead of having both of Beef. If the ladies can put up with such entertainment, and will submit to partake of it on plates, once tin but now Iron (not become so by the labor of scowering) I shall be happy to see them.

—In an invitation for two officers' wives to dine at West Point. (16 August)

{ 1780 }

1. It is not a custom with me to keep money to look at.

—In a letter to stepson John Parke Custis counseling on investments. (20 January)

{ 1783 }

1. The Army, as usual are without Pay; and a great part of the Soldiery without Shirts; and though the patience of them is equally threadbare, the States seem perfectly indifferent to their cries. In a word, if one was to hazard for them an opinion, upon this subject, it would be, that the Army had contracted such a habit of encountering distress and difficulties, and of living without money, that it would be impolitic and injurious to introduce other customs in it!

—In a letter to Major General John Armstrong of the Pennsylvania militia. (10 January)

2. On the President's observing that "Mr. Morris had his Hands Full," the General replied at the same instant, "He wished he had his Pockets full, too."

—Congressman David Howell reporting to Governor William Greene of Rhode Island about dining with General Washington at Princeton and responding to Elias Boudinot, President of Congress, observing that treasurer Robert Morris could not respond to complaints about the Army not being paid. (September)

{ 1784 }

1. The *Operator* is partial to his own performances, and the *Operatees*, in general, are inclined to compli-

ment, or having submitted to the *Operations,* are somewhat unwilling to expose the truth.

—In a letter to Richard Varick, sympathizing with Varick's having been operated on by a quack dentist. (22 February)

{ 1785 }

1. I am so hackneyed to the touches of the Painters pencil, that I am *now* altogether at their beck, and sit like Patience on a monument whilst they are delineating the lines of my face—It is a proof among others of what habit and custom can effect—At first I was as impatient at the request, and as restive under the operation, as a Colt is of the Saddle—The next time, I submitted very reluctantly but with less flouncing— Now, no dray moves more readily to the Thill than I do to the Painters Chair.

—Acknowledging a request from Francis Hopkinson that he sit for portrait artist Robert E. Pine. (16 May)

2. Without some stop can be put to the cutting and clipping of money, our Dollars, pistareens etc. will be converted, as Teague says, into *five* quarters.

—In letter to William Grayson discussing the need to prevent counterfeiting. (22 August)

{ 1786 }

1. Though young, he follows what one may suppose to be the example of his late Royal Master, who

cannot, though past his grand climacteric, perform seldom or without more majestic solemnity than he does.—However, I am not without hope that when he becomes a little better acquainted with republican enjoyments, he will amend his manners and fall into a better and more expeditious mode of doing business—

—In a letter to neighbor William Fitzhugh describing the jackass sent as gift from Charles the Third of Spain. (15 May)

{ 1787 }

1. Philip Bater for, and in consideration of the covenant herein, hereafter, mentioned, doth promise and agree to serve the said George Washington, for the term of one year, as a Gardner, and that he will, during said time, conduct himself soberly, diligently and honestly, that he will faithfully and industriously perform all, and every part of his duty as a Gardner, to the best of his knowledge and abilities, and that he will not, at any time, suffer himself to be disguised with liquor, except on the times hereafter mentioned. In consideration of these things being well and truly performed on the part of the said Philip Bater, the said George Washington doth agree to allow him . . . four Dollars at Christmas, with which he may be drunk 4 days and 4 nights; two Dollars at Easter to effect the same purpose; two Dollars also at Whitsuntide, to be drunk two days; a Dram in the morning, and a drink of Grog at Dinner or at Noon.

—In the handwriting of nephew G.A. Washington, this contract is signed by both the gardener and George Washington. (12 April)

2. General Washington presents his respectful compliments to Mrs. Powell, and would, with great pleasure, have made one of a party for the *School* for *Scandal* this evening had not everything been arranged, and Mr. Gouverneur Morris and himself on the point of stepping into the Carriage for a fishing expedition. ... The General can but regret that matters have turned out so unluckily, after waiting so long to receive a lesson in the School for Scandal.

—Turning down an invitation to attend a performance of R.B. Sheridan's *School for Scandal* with Eliza Powell. (30 July)

{ 1789 }

1. There can be at least *one* good reason adduced for my not dining out; to wit never having been asked to do so.

—In a letter to neighbor David Stuart explaining his social life as president. (26 July)

2. He with a degree of good humour, told his informant, and others that were present, that the Britons complained to Dr. Franklin of the ill usage their troops met with at Lexington battle by the Yankies getting behind stone walls, and firing at them; the Doctor replied, by asking them whether there were not two sides to the wall.

—*Gazette of the United States,* on the President's visit to the Lexington battlefield. (16 December)

{ 1791 }

1. This place is less than Hallifax, but more lively and thriving. . . . We were received at this place by as good a salute as could be given with one piece of artillery.

—Journal entry during tour of the South at Tarboro, North Carolina.

2. There being no Episcopal Minister present in the place, I went to hear morning Service performed in the Dutch reformed Church—which, being in that language not a word of which I understood I was in no danger of becoming a proselyte to its religion by the eloquence of the Preacher.

—Diary entry at York, Pennsylvania. (3 July)

{ 1797 }

1. Dispairing of hearing what may be said of him, if he should really go off in an apoplectic or any other fit (for he thinks all fits that issue in death are worse than a love fit, or a fit of laughter, and many other kinds which he could name) he is glad to hear beforehand, what will be said of him on that occasion; conceiving that nothing extra will happen between this and then, to make a change in his character—for better, or for worse—and besides, as he has entered into an engage-

ment with Mr. (Robert) Morris and several other gentlemen not to quit the theatre of this world before the year 1800, it may be relied upon, that no breach of contract shall be laid to him on that account; unless dire necessity should bring it about maugre all his exertions to the contrary. In that case, he shall hope they would do by him, as he would by them, excuse it: at present there seems to be no danger of his giving them the slip, as neither his health, nor spirits, were ever in greater flow, notwithstanding, he adds, he is descending, and has almost reached the bottom of the hill—or in other words, the shades below.

—Martha Washington quoting her husband in a letter to friend Elizabeth Powel. (18 December)

2. If the ideas of the possessor of them with respect to (enamoured love) have been of the Romantic order to have given them the warmth, which was not inherent, they might have been consigned to the flames.

—In letter to Mrs. Powel, who told him she had found love letters of his to Mrs. Washington in a desk drawer. (26 March)

3. As he sat at table after dinner, the fire behind him was too large and hot. He complained, and said he must remove. A gentleman observed it behoved the General to stand fire. "Yes," said Washington, "but it does not look well for a General to receive the fire behind."

—William Thornton recollecting Washington in retirement.

{ 1798 }

1. He observed that we had begun the session in very Cool Weather, he hoped that we would Keep Cool through the whole session.

—Congressman William Shepard, Massachusetts, reporting on a congressional delegation to the ex-president, called back to lead the armed forces against a threatened French invasion. (1 December)

2. "Did you know," Thomas Law asked him, "James Jones, who was recently killed in a duel by Brockholst Livingston?" "I believe I have seen him, but I was never on intimate terms with him." "They say that the shot that he fired at his opponent had grazed his nose." "How could he miss it?" replied the General. "You know Livingston's nose—what a target!"

—Polish visitor J.U. Niemcewicz reporting a conversation at Mount Vernon in June.

3. They spoke of the offices that were going to be built for the departments—the expense of it is estimated at 96,000 dollars. They discussed at length the difficulty that there would be to finish enough houses to lodge [congressmen in the new Federal City]. General Washington said jokingly, "Oh well, they can camp out. The Representatives in the first line, the Senate in the

second, the President with all his suite in the middle."
—Ibid.

{ 1799 }

1. And pray, my good Sir, what part of the $800,000 have come to your share? —As you are high in Office, I hope you did not disgrace yourself in the acceptance of a paltry bribe.— A 100,000 dollars perhaps.

—In a letter teasing Secretary of War James McHenry about press reports of bribing government officials by British spies. (11 August)

2. General Washington told me, that he never was so much annoyed by mosquitoes in any part of America as in Skenesborough, for they used to bite through the thickest boot.

—A British traveler reporting Washington's explanation of American mosquito power.

{ 1811 }

1. A greater loss than themselves, was that of the arms and ammunition they took away with them. I very well recollect, that it was found necessary to post a guard at Kingsbridge to stop the fugitives; and that upon one of them being arrested with a number of "notions" in a bag, there was found among them, a cannon ball, which, he said, he was taking home to his mother, for the purpose of pounding mustard.

—Alexander Graydon quoting Washington's recollection of his retreat from Long Island and New York City in the early days of the war.

{ 1817 }

1. A member made a motion that congress should be restricted to a standing army not exceeding 5,000, at any one time. General Washington, who, being chairman, could not offer a motion, whispered to a member from Maryland, to amend the motion, by providing that no foreign enemy should invade the United States, at any one time, with more than 3,000 troops.

—A Virginia legislator passing on an anecdote from a delegate to the Constitutional Convention of 1787. (11 April)

{ 1836 }

1. He called upon me to ask a blessing before meat. When the cloth was about to be removed, he returned thanks himself. Mrs. Washington, with a smile, said: "My dear, you forgot that you had a clergyman dining with you today." With equal pleasantness he replied: "My dear, I wish clergymen, and all men, to know that I am not a *graceless* man."

—Discussing Washington's religion, E.C. McGuire alludes to this traditional anecdote, recorded by eyewitness Rev. William McWhir.

{ 1853 }

1. General Washington was extremely punctual. His cabinet councils were appointed to meet him precisely at eleven o'clock on set days. On such occasions General Hamilton was usually latest and after the time; then he would bustle, and drawing out his watch exclaim it had deceived him. This occurred a number of times, when the General effectually prevented it by rising and looking firmly on General Hamilton and saying, "Sir, you must provide yourself a new watch, or I a new Secretary."

—A remark reported by Philadelphia antiquarian John F. Watson, who interviewed survivors of the Revolution.

{ 1856 }

1. When sitting there with the family, a toad passed near to where I was conversing with General Washington; which led him to ask me if I had ever observed this reptile swallow a firefly. Upon my answering in the negative, he told me that he had; and that, from the thinness of the skin of the toad, he had seen the light of the firefly after it had been swallowed. This was a new, and to me a surprising, fact in natural history.

—Boston merchant Thomas Handasyd Perkins's memoir recording one of Washington's tall tales told on Mount Vernon's porch.

{ 1877 }

1. Monsieur Volney, who has become so celebrated in his works, need only be named in order to be known in whatever part of the United States he may travel.

—Samuel Breck's memoirs recollecting Washington's response to the request by French radical C.F.C. Volney for a letter of introduction.

2. "The President of the United States presents his best respects to the Governor, and has the honor to inform him that he shall be at home till two o'clock. The President need not express the pleasure it will give him to see the Governor; but at the same time he most earnestly begs that the Governor will not hazard his health on the occasion."

—Breck's recording of the President's reply when he visited Massachusetts in 1789. Governor John Hancock in claiming illness as excuse for not welcoming him formally was actually asserting that states' rights required the President to visit the Governor first.

{ 1931 }

1. On an undated letter from a person who tried to borrow 500 pounds on the strength of a remarkable vision that came to him in a dream, Washington wrote, "From Mr. Thomas Bruff, without date and without Success."

—John C. Fitzpatrick, editing Washington's papers at the Library of Congress, uncovered this endorsement.

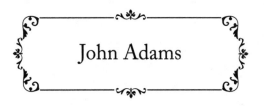

John Adams

JOHN ADAMS
LAUGHING

⌒᷅⌒

NOT ONE OF our better known presidents, John Adams takes luster from the reflected light of his remarkable wife Abigail. In his own time, the press would speak of her as "Madame President," while his name gradually paled even before that of their illustrious son John Quincy Adams. Yet John Adams remained unrelenting in pursuit of his own fame, trying to set the record straight on his role in the Revolution and as the nation's second president. In newspaper articles and correspondence, he wrote his side of the story in a style that reflected a mind that was anything but dull.

His style now seems oddly modern in being direct, self-dramatizing, and colloquial, sometimes to the point of being vulgar. In reply to the British ambassador's complaint about the Yanks—"Why should they wish to rip open our belly, the belly of their mother?"— Adams wrote: "The child would never have thought of hurting the mother, if she had not plucked the nipple from the boneless gums, and attempted to dash the brains out."[1]

The spontaneity of such style may have derived from his refusal to revise in cold blood what had been written at white heat. In fact, he confessed to his friend Benjamin Rush that he could not compose formal speeches because, lacking the patience to revise, correct, amend, polish, refine, or otherwise embellish, "I understand it not."[2] If he had followed Washington's practice of revising earlier writings, we would have lost such Adamsian gems as the image of a farmer and wife and four children "all pigged in together" or the sound of "the tyrannical bell that dongled me out of my house every morning."[3]

It would be nice to find that Adams was born with this sense of humorous style, but his diaries and correspondence show a constant concern for cultivating it. He would record the stories told by other people, often describe the way the stories were told, and even analyze them. Adams repeats Franklin's tale of the Spanish mystic in Hell complaining that there were so few kings there; the guardian devil sighs, "Here are all the Kings that ever reigned," complaining in turn, "What the Devil would the Man have?" Then Adams comments on Franklin's tale that Dr. Watts more charitably described Heaven—"Here and there I see a King"—"This seems to imply that We see a King upon Earth."

Franklin, a favorite model, usually needed no comment. Adams simply records a story or fable. He tells about the amateur scientist immersed in experiment being called to dinner:

"Sir, dinner is on Table."

"Dinner! Pox! Pough! But what have you for dinner?"

"Ham and Chickens."

"Ham! And must I break the chain of my thoughts to go down and gnaw a morsel of a damn'd Hogs Arse?"

No comment.

Yet one of the few instances of Adams in the act of revising appears in a diary entry for 20 May 1778 and again in his autobiography a quarter-century later. The tale is about the encounter of a tailor and horse thief in jail:

Diary	*Autobiography*
The Taylor told the other, his Story. The other enquired why he had not taken such a Road and assumed such a Disguise, and why he had not disguised the Horse?"	The Taylor told the other, his Story. The other enquired why he had not taken such a Road and assumed such a Disguise, and why he had not disguised the Horse?"
"I did not think of it."	"I did not think of it."
"Who are you? and what has been your Employment?"	"Did not think of it? Who are you? and what has been your Employment?"

Though so slight as to be almost overlooked, the revision sharpens the dialogue, making it more realistic, more Franklinian, more the language of common people in conversation.

The same concern may be seen in random sampling. Adams records the story about the local yokel asking a market girl for a little "jigging" in its sexual sense. She asks in all innocence, "What is that?" and he answers "It will make you fat!" "Pray," says she, "jigg my Mare.

She's miserably lean." He even tries to recapture an Admiral's "coarse, low, vulgar" speech overheard: "My wifes d----d Arse is so broad that she and I can't sit in a Chariot together."

When friends asked him to write his life story, he said, "My Life is already written in my Letter books."[4] He retained copies of his correspondence over the years, including love letters to Abigail Adams, another repository for practicing jests. When still Abigail Smith, she asked him for a list of her imperfections. He sent an inventory of half a dozen, including her pigeon-toed walk and her habit of sitting with legs crossed, which, he said, came from thinking too much. In turn, he confessed needing improvement in such social graces as "the nobler Arts of smutt, Double Entendre, and Mimickry of Dutchmen and Negroes" and vowed to keep "a Register of all the stories, Squibbs, Gibes, and Compliments, I shall hear thro the whole Week," in order to match those of her other beaus.[5]

His letters do indeed constitute a register. They tell about the sailor hit by cannon shot, splattering "blood and brains" all over a nearby officer, who complains, "What Business that fellow had here with so much Brains in his Head." And they tell about the Frenchman being guillotined, crying, "Vive la répub—" as the head is cut off, "hopping and bouncing and rolling" while finishing, "—lique." The letters from France show increasing sophistication. Jests about jigging give way to more subtle remarks by the German ambassador who "could not bear St. Paul, he was so severe against forni-cation." As our second president, he responded to a rumor that he had sent C.C. Pinckney on a mission to France to procure a couple of girls apiece. "If this be true," he wrote, "General Pinckney has kept them all for himself and cheated me out of my two."

Whether in diary, autobiography, or correspondence, Adams's favorite form of humor seems to have been what he called "humbugging." He admired con men like the Frenchman who advertised a flea powder that brought ladies flocking. When the con man told them to catch the flea between your thumb and forefinger, then pour the powder down their throats, the ladies asked, "Since you have it between thumb and finger, why not squeeze it to death?" The con man replied, "That would do as well."

He can deceive even himself. Visiting London, he is flattered to find a street named John Adams, only to dis-cover later that the street was named after an architect of the same name. He relished the role of straight man. When bantering with a French lady about his name, he assumed a grave air when she asked if, given his name, he derived directly from the first couple. She said she had been long intrigued by how the first couple "found out the Art of lying together." Adams suggested that it was a natural quality, like the attraction of magnets or electricity. "Well," said she, "I know not how it was, but this I do know—it is a very happy shock."

In recounting that story in his autobiography, Adams

comments on what he should have said in repartee, but in tranquillity recollects that "her Ladyship and all the Company would only have thought it Pedantry and Bigotry," a sign that a quarter-century later he was still analyzing his own performance. Yet clearly the humor of his old age shows a marked advance, relying on apt metaphor or imagery rather than simple word play. Noah Webster visited the old man to ask about his health. "I inhabit a weak, frail, decayed tenement," said Adams, "open to the winds, and broken in upon by the storms." Then he adds, "What is worse, from all I can learn, the landlord does not intend to repair."[6]

It was no fault of John Adams that posterity enjoyed so little of his humor. Grandson Charles Francis Adams edited his works in the mid-1850s, remaining close to the text but omitting much from the diaries and autobiography and making what he called "a rigid selection" from the letters, sometimes substituting a more formal style for the colloquial, if vulgar, expressions that gave us John Adams speaking to people rather than to posterity. Fortunately, newly edited Adams Papers from Harvard University Press ongoing since 1961 will restore the John Adams that Abigail knew.

NOTES TO ADAMS INTRODUCTION

1. *Correspondence of the Late President Adams . . . in the Boston Patriot* (1809), letter 34 dated 5 September 1809, 314.

2. *The Spur of Fame,* edited by Douglass Adair and John Shutz (San Marino: Huntington Library Press, 1966) letter dated 28 August 1811, 194.

3. "Butterfield's Adams," *William and Mary Quarterly* 19 (1962), 246.

4. *Diary and Autobiography,* ed. Lyman Butterfield (Cambridge: Harvard University Press, 1961), I:LXX.

5. *Book of Abigail and John,* ed. Lyman Butterfield, et al. (Cambridge: Harvard University Press, 1975), 41–43.

6. Charles W. March, *Reminiscences of Congress* (New York: Baker & Scribner, 1850), 62.

{ 1759 }

1. They told of the wickedest jokes that had been put upon Nat Hurd, by some fellows in Boston, who found out that he had such a Girl at his shop, at such a time. One went to him and pretended to make a confidant of him. "Oh god, what shall I do? That Girl, her, has given me the Clap." That scared him and made him cry, "Oh damn her, what shall I do? I saw her such a Night. I am. . . ." He went to the Doctor and was salivated for the Clap. Then they sent him before Justice Phillips, then before Justice Tyler, in short they played upon him till they provoked him so that he swore he would beat the Brains out of the first man that came into his shop, to plague him with his. . . .

—Diary record of a practical joke by some of his friends. (Spring)

2. Ephraim Thayer told a Story the other day that he saw a small ground Squirrell run away with two large

Ears. He introduced it with a solemn Train of Circumstances. He raised a great deal of Corn, and could not imagine how it went. He could not suspect any of his Neighbours, and he thought no Creature but Man could take it off so fast. At last he lay and watched it and soon found that the squirrells were the Thieves for he saw one single ground squirrell run out of his fold with two ears. —This Pun.

—Another diary record about the same time.

3. F. Morris said to him, "You are going Sir to Abraham's Bosom, but I don't know but I shall reach there first." —"Ay if you are agoing there, I don't want to go."

—About the same time, speaking of "Father" Flynt, an old tutor at Harvard.

4. Two Countrymen were disputing which did the most good, the Sun or the Moon. One of them asserted that the Moon did the most because that shines in the Night, when without that, we should be in absolute Darkness, but the Sun never shone till it was broad day light, as light as Day . . . when there was no need of it.

—An entry quoting Rev. Ebenezer Gay. (Summer)

{ 1760 }

1. He attacked an old Squaw one day (who) made answer, "You poor smitten Boy, you with your Knife in your Tail and your Loaf on your Back, did your Mother born you so?"

—An entry quoting his father's stories about a

hunchbacked lawyer he'd known as a youth. (November)

2. A Market Girl whom he overtook, and asked to let him jigg her, answered by asking, "What is that? What good will that do?" He replied, "It will make you fat!" "Pray be so good then," says the Girl, "as to Jigg my Mare. She's miserably lean."

—Another of his father's stories.

{ 1762 }

1. The story of R. Bicknal's Wife is a very clever one. She said, when she was married she was very anxious, she feared, she trembled, she could not go to Bed. But she recollected she had put her Hand to the Plow and could not look back, so she mustered up her Spirits, committed her soul to God and her Body to B. Bicknal and into Bed she leaped—and in the Morning she was amazed, she could not think for her Life what it was that had scared her so.

—Entry recording Dr. Cotton Tufts telling "some good matrimonial stories. (30 November)

{ 1763 }

1. My great grandfather was one of Oliver Cromwell's men, and I've heard it, in our family by tradition, that good, pious, larnt Mr. Hugh Peters us'd to say, it would never be good times, till the nation got rid of 150.—Sumbody asked what he ment by 150?—He said three L's.—and when he was asked what he ment

by three L's, he said, the Lords, the Levites and the Lawyers.

—In a Boston *Evening Post* letter, under the pen name Humphrey Ploughjogger, replying to a letter by "U," Adams himself. (5 September)

2. I've read abundance in my day, but I did not begin to read a grate deel till I was matter of 35, and I cant larn to spell nicely. But since I married this second wife, that is a young woman, I don't love to go to bed so soon as she does, so I read and rite a world now, and I do spell better and better.

—Ibid.

{ 1767 }

1. My neighbour Worldly had a Yoke of Oxen, that he was going to sell to a Stranger, for a fine Yoke of working Cattle, but seven Years old, but the Stranger happen'd to go on one side a little, and sees my Neighbour Worldly's Negro Man Toney, and asks him about them Oxen. "Oh," says Toney, "they are as nice a Yoke of Oxen to work as ever stood under a Yoke. I have drove 'em myself this 12 Years, and never drove so good a Yoke as they are." Upon this the Stranger comes back to my Neighbour, told him what Toney had said, and would not have the Cattle. My Neighbour was very wroth, and after he got Home, he scolds at Toney very sadly. "You told the Man that you had driven the Oxen 12 Years, and I told him they were but 7 Year old, you

Blockhead," says my Neighbour. "Oh, Master," says Toney, "I'm very sorry. *I see now where I mist it.*"

—In a letter, Humphrey Ploughjogger is reminded of "a comical Thing that happened tother Day in our Town". (19 January)

{ 1771 }

1. The Duke of York was in a Battle at Sea, a cannon Ball hit a Mans Head and dashed his Blood and Brains in the Dukes Face and Eyes. The Duke started, and leaped quite out of the Rank. The Officer, who commanded, said, "Pray your Highness don't be frightened." The Duke replied, "Oh sir, I am not frightened but I wonder what Business that fellow had here with so much Brains in his Head."

—A diary story. (25 April)

2. Somebody knowing they all had a great Esteem of Bob Temple begged him to interpose and use his Influence to make Peace. At last he was persuaded, and went in among the Persons, and one of the first Steps he took to make Peace was to give one of the Persons a Blow in the Face with his fist.

—Ibid., telling about Cambridge gentlemen quarreling.

3. He said the Defence put him in Mind of the Answer of a Young Fellow to the Father of a Girl. The Father caught the young Fellow in naked Bed with his Daughter. The old Man between Grief and Rage broke

out into Reproaches.— "You wretch, what do you mean by trying to get my Daughter with Child?" The Young fellow answered him, "I try to get your Daughter with Child! I was trying not to get her with Child."

—Ibid., recording a story told privately by Caleb Strong.

4. A Dog and a Toad were to run a Race, and if the Dog reached the Goal first, the World was to continue innocent and happy, but if the Toad should outstrip the Dog, the world was to become sinful and miserable. Everybody thought there could be no danger. But in the Midst of the Career the Dog found a bone by the Way and stopped to knaw it, and while he was interrupted by his Bone, the Toad, constant in his Malevolence, hopped on, reached the Mark, and spoiled the World.

—Entry quoting Dr. Samuel Cooper's slave Glasgow on how evil was introduced into the world. (14 May)

5. He called at a Tavern in the fall of the Year for a Dram. The Landlord asked him two Coppers for it. The next Spring, happening at the same House, he called for another and had three Coppers to pay for it.— "How is this, Landlord," says he, "last fall you asked but two Coppers for a Glass of Rum, now you ask three."— "Oh!" says the Landlord, "it costs me a good deal to keep Rum over Winter. It is as expensive to keep an Hogshead of Rum over Winter as a Horse."— "Ay," says the Indian, "I cant see through that. He won't

eat so much Hay— maybe he Drink as much Water."

—Entry, as instance of "sheer Wit, pure Satyre, and true Humour" in the repartee of a Connecticut Indian. (10 November)

{ 1772 }

1. Erving met Parson Morehead near his Meeting House.— "You have a fine Steeple, and Bell," says he, "to your Meeting House now."—"Yes, by the Liberality of Mr. Hancock and the Subscriptions of some other Gentlemen. We have a very hansome and convenient House of it at last."—"But what has happened to the Vane, Mr. Morehead, it dont traverse, it has pointed the same Way these three Weeks."—"Ay, I did not know it, I'll see about it." —Away goes Morehead, storming among his Parish, and the Tradesmen, who had built the Steeple, for fastening the Vane so that it could not move. The Tradesmen were alarmed, and went to examine it, but soon found the fault was not in the Vane but the Weather, the Wind having sat very constantly at East, for three Weeks before.

—Entry retelling James Otis, Jr.'s story about Colonel John Erving's practical joke. (27 October)

{ 1774 }

1. Mr. Willing told us a Story of a Lawyer here, who the other Day, gave him upon the Bench the following Answer, to a Question Why the Lawyers were so increased.

"You ask me why Lawyers so much are increas'd
Tho most of the Country already are fleec'd
The Reason I'm sure is most strikingly plain
The Sheep are oft sheared yet the Wool grows
    again
And tho you may think e'er so odd of the Matter
The oft'ner they're fleeced, the Wool grows the
    better
Thus downy-chin'd Boys as oft I have heard
By frequently shaving obtain a large Beard."

—Entry repeating Judge Thomas Willing's recitation in Philadelphia of Richard Peters' verses. (11 September)

{ 1775 }

1. Somebody said, there was nobody on our side but the Almighty. The Doctor who is a native of Switzerland, and speaks but broken English, quickly replied, "Dat is enough—Dat is enough," and turning to me, says he, "It puts me in mind of a fellow who once said, 'The Catholics have on their side the Pope, and the King of France and the King of Spain, and the King of Sardinia, and the King of Poland and the Emperor of Germany etc. etc. etc. But as to them poor Devils the Protestants, they have nothing on their side but God Almighty.' "

—Letter to his wife, including a bon mot from Dr. J. Zubly. (1 October)

{ 1776 }

1. At Brunswick, but one bed could be procured for Dr. Franklin and me, in a Chamber little larger than the bed, without a Chimney and with only one small Window. The Window was open, and I, who was an invalid and afraid of the Air in the night . . . shut it close. "Oh!" says Franklin, "don't shut the Window. We shall be suffocated." I answered I was afraid of the Evening Air. Dr. Franklin replied, "The Air within this Chamber will soon be, and indeed is now worse than that without Doors. Come! open the Window and come to bed, and I will convince you. I believe you are not acquainted with my Theory of Colds." Opening the Window and leaping into Bed, I said I had read his Letters to Dr. Cooper in which he had advanced, that Nobody ever got cold by going into a cold Church, or any other cold Air. . . . However I had so much curiosity to hear his reasons, that I would run the risque of a cold. The Doctor then began an harrangue, upon Air and cold and Respiration and Perspiration, with which I was so much amused that I soon fell asleep, and left him and his Philosophy together. But I believe they were equally sound and insensible, within a few minutes after me, for the last Words I heard were pronounced as if he was more than half asleep.

—Diary entry recording an episode at New Brunswick, New Jersey, while Adams, along with Franklin and Edward Rutledge, journeyed to negotiate with the British at New York. (9 September)

{ 1778 }

1. A Frenchman in London advertised an infallible Remedy against Fleas. The Ladies all flocked to purchase the Powder. But after they had bought it, one of them asked for Directions to Use it.—"Madame," says the Frenchman, "you must catch the Flea, and squeeze him between your Fingers until he gape, then you must put a little of this Powder in his Mouth, and I will be responsible he never will bite you again."— "But," says the Lady, "when I have him between my Fingers, why may I not rub him to death?"—"Oh, Madam dat will do just as well den!"

—Entry recording a shipboard story told by Captain Samuel Tucker en route to France. (29 March)

2. One of the most elegant Ladies at Table, young and handsome, tho married to a Gentleman in the Company, was pleased to address her discourse to me. Mr. Bondfield must interpret the Speech which he did in these Words: "Mr. Adams, by your Name I conclude you are descended from the first Man and Woman, and probably in your family may be preserved the tradition which may resolve a difficulty which I could never explain. I never could understand how the first Couple found out the Art of lying together?" Whether her phrase was, *"L'Art de se coucher ensemble"* or any other more energetic, I know not, but Mr. Bondfield rendered it by that I have mentioned. To me, whose Acquaintance with Women had been confined to

America, where the manners of the Ladies were universally characterized at that time by Modesty, Delicacy and Dignity, this question was surprising and shocking; but though I believe I at first blushed, I was determined not to be disconcerted. I thought it would be as well for once to set a brazen face against a brazen face and answer a fool according to her folly, and accordingly composing my countenance into an Ironical Gravity I answered her, "Madame My Family resembles the first Couple both in the name and in their frailties so much that I have no doubt We are descended from that in Paradise. But the Subject was perfectly understood by Us, whether by tradition I could not tell: I rather thought it was by Instinct, for there was a Physical quality in us resembling the Power of Electricity or of the Magnet, by which when a Pair approached within a striking distance they flew together like the Needle to the Pole or like two Objects in electric Experiments." When this Answer was explained to her, she replied, "Well I know not how it was, but this I know— it is a very happy Shock."

—Recalling an experience at Bordeaux, France. (April)

3. An officer petitioned him, to make him a Captain of his Life Guard. The Cardinal answered that he had no Occasion for any other Guard than his Tutelary Angell. "Ah! Sir," said the Officer, "your Enemies will put him to flight with a few drops of holy Water."—It was a wonder that something worse had not happened to the Officer, for his insinuation was nothing less than

that the Devil was the Cardinal's only tutelary Angell.

—The autobiography recording a story by Jacques Barbeau Dubourg about Cardinal Mazarine. (April)

4. He had chosen for his Valet, the stoutest Grenadier in his Army who frequently plaid at Hot Cockles with another of his Domesticks who was named Stephen. The Marshal one day stooped down to look out of a Window with one of his hands upon his back. The Grenadier, coming suddenly into the Chamber, raised his gigantic arm and with his brawny palm gave his master a furious blow upon his hand upon his back. The Marshal drew himself in and looked at the Grenadier, who the moment he saw it was his Master fell upon his Knees in despair, begging for Mercy "for he thought it was Stephen."— "Well," said the Marshal, rubbing his hand which was tingling with the Smart, "if it had been Stephen, you ought not to have struck so hard" and said no more upon the Subject.

—A Dubourg anecdote from the autobiography this one about Marshal De Turenne and his stoutest grenadier, his valet. (April)

5. Voltaire and Franklin were both present, and there presently arose a general Cry that Monsieur Voltaire and Monsieur Franklin should be introduced to each other. This was done and they bowed and spoke to each other. This was no Satisfaction. There must be something more. Neither of our Philosophers seemed to divine what was wished or expected. They however took each other by the hand. . . . But this was not

enough. The Clamour continued, untill the explanation came out *"Il faut s'embrasser, a la francoise."* The two Aged Actors upon this great Theatre of Philosophy and frivolity then embraced each other by hugging one another in their Arms and kissing each others cheeks, and then the tumult subsided. And the Cry immediately spread through the whole Kingdom and I suppose over all Europe . . . "How charming it was! Oh! it was enchanting to see Solon and Sophocles embracing!"

—Describing the meeting of Franklin and Voltaire at the French Academy of Sciences. (29 April)

6. A Spanish Writer of certain Vissions of Hell, relates that a certain Devil who was civil and well bred, shewed him all the Departments in the Place—among others the Department of Deceased Kings. The Spaniard was much pleased at so illustrious a Sight, and after viewing them for some time, said he should be glad to see the Rest of them.—"The Rest!?" said the Daemon. "Here are all the Kings that ever reigned upon Earth from the Creation of it to this day, what the Devil would the Man have?"

—Diary entry recording a Franklin tale. (8 May)

7. A certain Taylor once stole an Horse, and was found out and committed to Prison, where he met another Person who had long followed the Trade of Horse Stealing. The Taylor told the other his Story. The other enquired why he had not taken such a Road and assumed such a Disguise, and why he had not disguised the Horse?—"I did not think of it."—"Who are you?

and what has been your Employment?"—"A Taylor."—
"You never stole a Horse before, I suppose in your
Life."—"Never."—"G-d d--n you, what Business had
you with Horse stealing? Why did you not content yourself with your Cabbage?"

—Entry recording another Franklin tale. (20 May)

8. Ah, no! Alas, alas, no! The ladies of this country, Madam, have an unaccountable passion for old age,
whereas our countrywomen, you know, Madam, have
rather a complaisance for youth, if I remember right.
This is rather unlucky for me, because here I have nothing to do but wish that I was seventy years old, and,
when I get back to America, I shall be obliged to wish
myself back again to five-and-twenty.

—In a letter replying to Mercy Warren, who asked
if he were as popular with the ladies as Franklin was. (15
December)

{ 1782 }

1. Dr. Franklin, upon my saying, the other day,
that I fancied he did not exercise so much as he was
wont, answered, "Yes, I walk a League every day in my
Chamber. I walk quick and for an hour, so that I go a
League. I make a Point of Religion of it." I replied, that
as the Commandment "Thou shalt not kill" forbids a
Man to kill himself as well as his Neighbor, it was man-
ifestly a Breach of the Sixth Commandment not to
exercise. So that he might easily prove it to be a religious
Point.

—Diary entry reporting a conversation with Franklin. (22 November)

{ 1783 }

1. The post-boy . . . carried us to the Adelphi buildings in the Strand. Whether it was the boy's cunning, or whether it was mere chance, I know not, but I found myself in a street which was marked John's Street. The postilion turned a corner, and I was in Adam's Street. He turned another corner, and I was in John Adam's Street! I thought, surely we are arrived in Fairy land.

—Concluding a series of reminiscences in the *Boston Patriot* recalling a visit to London in October. (20 October)

2. I was received in State. Two great Chairs before the Fire, one of which was destined for me, the other for his Excellency. Two Secretaries of Legation, men of no Small Consequence Standing Upright in the middle of the Room, without daring to Sit, during the whole time I was there, and whether they are not yet upright upon their legs I know not. . . . He began soon to ask me Questions about America and her Tobacco, and I was surprized to find that with a pittance of Italian and a few French Words which he understands, We could so well understand each other. "We make Tobacco in Tripoli," said his Excellency, "but it is too Strong. Your American Tobacco is better." By this Time, one of his secretaries or *upper servants* brought two Pipes ready

filled and lighted. The longest was offered to his Excellency. It is long since I took a Pipe but as it would be unpardonable to be wanting in Politeness in so ceremonious an Interview, I took the Pipe with great Complacency, placed the Bowl upon the Carpet, for the Stem was fit for a Walking Cane, and I believe more than two Yards in length, and Smoaked in aweful Pomp, reciprocating Whiff for Whiff, with his Excellency, untill the Coffee was brought in. His Excellency took a Cup, after I had taken one, and alternately Sipped at his Coffee and whiffed at his Tobacco, and I wished he would take a Pinch in turn from his Snuff box for Variety; and I followed the Example with such Exactness and Solemnity that the two secretaries appeared in Raptures and the superiour of them who speaks a few Words of French cryed out in Extacy, *"Monsieur votes etes un Turk!"*

—In letter from London to Jefferson in Paris reporting on a visit to the ambassador from Tripoli. (17 February)

{ 1786 }

1. The Wit attempted to divert himself, by asking the Scot if he knew the immense Distance to Heaven? It was so many Millions of Diameters of the Solar System, and a Cannon Ball would be so many Thousand Years in running there. "I don't know the Distance nor the Time," says the Scot, "but I know it will not take you a Millionth part of the Time to go to Hell."

—Diary entry recording Joseph Paice's story about a scientist trying to humble a Scot. (6 July)

{ 1790 }

1. The History of our Revolution will be one continued Lye from one end to the other. The essence of the whole will be that "Dr. Franklins electrical Rod smote the Earth and out sprung General Washington. That Franklin electrified him with his rod—and thence forward these two conducted all the Policy, Negotiations, Legislatures and War." These Lines contain the whole Fable Plot and Catastrophy. If this Letter should be preserved, and read an hundred years hence the Reader will say, "The envy of this J.A. could not bear to think of the Truth! He ventured to scribble to Rush, as envious as himself, Blasphemy that he dared not speak when he lived. But Barkers at the Sun and Moon are always Silly Curs."

—In a letter to Dr. Benjamin Rush. (4 April)

{ 1797 }

1. The good President laughed, then considering his enormous height said to him, "You should have been born in the states of the King of Prussia. You would have been the ornament of his guards." "Would I have been the second in his kingdom, I would not wish to have been born there," the tanner said to him. "Nor I," answered the President, "would I have been the first."
—Polish visitor Julian Niemcewicz reporting dialogue

at a dinner between President Adams and Mr. Goss, "6 feet tall, over 70 years old, tanner by trade and prattler by habit." (8 November)

{ 1800 }

1. I do declare upon my honor, if this be true, General Pinckney has kept them all for himself and cheated me out of my two.

—In a letter to William Tudor commenting on a rumor that he had sent C.C. Pinckney to England to procure for them two girls each. (13 December)

{ 1804 }

1. A German ambassador once told me he "could not bear St. Paul, he was so severe against fornication."

—In a letter to F.A. Vanderkemp on music. (3 March)

{ 1812 }

1. When I hear a man boast of his indifference to public censure, I think of Henry the Fourth. A braggadocio in his army solicited advancement and command, and to enforce his pretensions, he extolled and exalted his own courage. "Sire, I know not what fear is, I never felt fear in my life."—"I presume then, Sir," said the good-natured monarch, "you never attempted to snuff a candle with your thumb and finger."

—In a letter to Dr. Benjamin Rush. (12 June)

2. Sam Adams' liberty was like the liberty of Parson Burr of Worcester, an ancestor of Aaron. The liberty of a man chained hand and foot in a dungeon: that is, a perfect liberty to stay there.

—In a letter to Rush. (1 August)

{ 1813 }

1. Upon some Occasion there was a complaint against him as a Justice of the Peace in the County of Worcester. He arrived in Boston and the Counsell sent for him, and interrogated him and threatened him. When he came down from the Counsell Chamber, one of his Brother Representatives asked him, "What can the matter be?"—"God damn them," said Chandler, "they talk of uncreating their Creator."

—In a letter to Jefferson discussing Judge John Chandler, "one of our New England Nobility" with great influence in the legislature. (12 July)

2. In 1775 Franklin made a morning Visit, at Mrs. Yards to Sam Adams and John. He was unusually loquacious. "Man, a rational Creature!" said Franklin. "Come let us suppose a rational Man. Strip him of all his Appetites, especially of his hunger and thirst. He is in his Chamber, engaged in making Experiments, or in pursuing some Problem. He is highly entertained. At this moment a Servant Knocks. "Sir dinner is on Table."—"Dinner! Pox! Pough! What have you for dinner?"—"Ham and Chickens."—"Ham! And must I

break the chain of my thoughts, to go down and knaw a morsel of a damn'd Hogs Arse? Put aside your Ham. I will dine tomorrow."

—In a letter to Jefferson. (15 November)

{ 1816 }

1. Brissot and some of his colleagues are said to have pronounced "Vive la répub—," when the guillotine has cut off the head, which hopping and bouncing and rolling has articulated the syllable "lique," after it was sundered from the shoulders.

—In a letter to F.A. Vanderkemp. (26 May)

2. The aged philosopher alighted from his coach at my door, at Auteuil, on an invitation to dinner. I never saw a more perfect picture of horror, terror, or grief than his countenance. I was shocked with surprise and compassion. He turned to his coachman and said, "You need not come for me. I will walk home." He then turned to me and said, "I will never enter the door of a coach again, at least if I cannot find a coachman who has the stone."

—In the same letter, talking about Franklin's last days in France, miserable from kidney stones and other ailments. (26 May)

{ 1817 }

1. The Parson and the Pedagogue lived much together, but were eternally disputing about Government

and Religion. One day, when the Schoolmaster had been more than commonly fanatical and declared, if he were a Monark, he would have but one Religion in his Dominions, the Parson cooly replied, "Cleverly! you would be the best Man in the World, if You had no Religion."

—In a letter to Jefferson, reminiscing about his old schoolmaster and preacher. (19 April)

{ 1820 }

1. When Harris was returned a Member of Parliament a Friend introduced him to Chesterfield whom he had never seen.—"So, Mr. Harris," said his Lordship, "you are a member of the House of Commons. You have written upon Universal and scientifick Grammar! You have written upon Art, upon Musick, Painting and Poetry! And what has the House of Commons to do with Art, or Musick, or Painting, or Poetry, or Taste?"—"Have not you written upon Virtue and Happiness?"—"I have indulged myself in Speculations upon those subjects."—"And what the devil has the House of Lords to do with either Happiness or Virtue?"

—In a letter to Jefferson, talking about writer Sir James Harris. (20 January)

2. While I was with him, and conversing on the common topics of the day, some one—a friend of his— came in and made particular enquiry of his health. "I am not well," he replied. "I inhabit a weak, frail, decayed

tenement; battered by the winds, and broken in upon by the storms; and from all I can learn, the landlord does not intend to repair."

—Daniel Webster recalls visiting Adams in his last days.

3. There was living in Albemarle, at the time of Jefferson's death, an enthusiastic democrat, who, admiring him beyond all men, thought that, by dying on the 4th of July, he had raised himself and his party one step higher in the temple of fame. Then came the news that John Adams had died on the same great day. Indignant at the bare suggestion of such a thing, he at first refused to believe it, and, when he could no longer discredit the news, exclaimed, in a passion, that "it was a damned Yankee trick."

—Jefferson's great-granddaughter, Sarah Randolph, recalling a Virginian's reaction to Adams' death. (July 1820)

Thomas Jefferson

THOMAS JEFFERSON
LAUGHING

✂

JEFFERSON was a man of letters. He estimated that in one year alone he composed about 1,267 of them, and over a lifetime his correspondence came close to 25,000 letters.[1] He did employ a secretary but answered his own mail, writing, he said, "from sunrise to breakfast,"[2] as though paying due reverence to the power of words.

Not all the letters were private, of course, for he earned an early reputation as "a masterly Pen"[3] (John Adams's words) in composing such national treasures as the Declaration of Independence, which he himself gave priority in listing achievements for his own epitaph: "Author of the Declaration of Independence, of the Statute of Virginia for religious freedom and Father of the University of Virginia." And he told his heirs: "Not a word more."[4]

While one of the youngest delegates to the Continental Congress, he had been named to the committee drafting the Declaration because of his reputation as penman of the Virginia legislature. Congress quibbled over every word. Franklin sustained him against the swarm of nitpickers by telling the tale of a hatter, John Thompson, whose new signboard, "John Thompson, Hatter, makes and Sells Hats for Ready Money," with an image of a hat, ends up as merely "John Thompson" with a hat subjoined.

The irony is that for years Jefferson had trained himself to revere brevity. "No stile of writing is so delightful as that which is all pith, which never omits a necessary word, nor uses an unnecessary one."[5] From student days, he had practiced "commonplacing," distilling whatever he read into précis form: "At first I could shorten it very little; but after a while I was able to put a page of a book into two or three sentences, without omitting any portion of the substance."[6]

Besides developing habits of close reading and cutting to the heart of the matter, commonplacing also helped develop Jefferson's concise style—"the most valuable of all talents, that of never using two words where one will do."[7] This compression could sometimes lead to incomprehensibility. Senator William Maclay said Jefferson "scattered information wherever he went"[8] but sometimes was hard to follow.

Maclay recounts the two of them in conference on establishing diplomatic service for overseas. Jefferson tried to set out the practical problems involved, saying, "It is better to take the highest of the lowest than the lowest of the highest." Maclay and the other conferees had trouble figuring out that he meant: "It is better to appoint a chargé with a handsome salary than a minister plenipotentiary with a small one."

That kind of statement, fitter for writing than speaking, was suited to Jefferson's epigrammatic wit, as in his saying that a professorship in mathematics was hereditary. A thinking man's wit, this style contrasts with Adams's when both write on the same subject.

Adams tells of being introduced as a colleague of Franklin's by a Parisian who urges his female companion to kiss Adams as Franklin's successor. She replies, "No, monsieur, he is too young." Adams rejoins, "You see I must wait patiently full thirty years before I can be so great a favorite." In similar circumstances, Jefferson says he watched Franklin being smothered by a Parisienne's kisses. Jefferson asks to share some of them. Franklin teases him: "You are too young a man"—and Jefferson adds not a word more.

This kind of compression surfaces in private correspondence, as in his writing to daughter Martha to ask for news of Monticello neighbors: "Who marry, who hang themselves because they cannot marry."[9] Still, he had to be circumspect in correspondence that would circulate widely, and the habitual practice of compressing coupled with the need for circumspection often resulted in a style inappropriately cold, as in advising Martha, "Determine never to be idle. No person will have occasion to complain of the want of time who never loses any."[10]

Other times, his style could be appropriately lush, eliciting from the romantic Maria Cosway, "Your letters . . . are so well wrote, so full of a thousand preaty things that it is not possible for me to Answer."[11] Sometimes it undercuts pathetic sentiment. After writing out a verse on growing old, he offers an old friend's plain prose: "He was tired of pulling off his shoes and stockings at night, and putting them on again in the morning."[12] Such facility in a broad range of writing styles seems natural in someone with Jefferson's reverence for the power of words to do more than convey information efficiently—to evoke feelings, to move men's minds.

One effect of this reverence is absence of wordplay and clear preference for brow-furrowing wit. Apologizing for composing draft legislation in simple language, he proposes having someone else translate it into language lawyers can understand. In proposing that at the Creation, Europe was merely a maiden effort, he calls the results "a crude production, before the maker knew his trade, or had made up his mind as to what he wanted." No knee-slapping humor here, only incisive comment.

This is not to say Jefferson was humorless. He enjoyed laughing at the absurdity of his own situation. When someone congratulated him at his inauguration, the President replied that he never congratulated a bridegroom till a year after the wedding. And when a lady at Madison's inaugural ball observed that Jefferson was the happier of the two, he told her, "I have got the burthen off my shoulders, while he has now got it on his."

Among friends he would also indulge in tall tales and shaggy dog stories that went nowhere. He teased serious John Quincy Adams with an anecdote about a Marseilles winemaker "who told him that he would make him any sort of wine he could name, and in any quantities, at six or eight sols the bottle. And though there should not be a drop of the genuine wine required in his composition yet it should so perfectly imitate the taste, that the most refined connoisseur should not be able to tell which was which." John Quincy Adams was confused.

The master of such teasing was his old friend Franklin. In fact, Jefferson was responsible for many of our favorite Franklin stories, as if the old man were his favorite hero of humor. It was Jefferson who told how the old man stood silently by as the French historian Abbé Raynal argued for the authenticity of Polly Baker's speech when prosecuted for the fifth time for having a bastard child. When Franklin could contain himself no longer and confessed writing it to fill columns in his newspaper, Raynal replied, "I had rather relate your stories than other men's truths."

His Franklin stories reveal much about Jefferson's attitudes. They reflect warm affection for his old friend, and, in comparison with stories about Washington and Adams, tell us what he thought of them, too. The

Washington stories are bitter, and those about Adams bemused, reflecting the attitude Jefferson expresses in his notes and autobiographical writings. In selection and style, they open a window into his emotions as well as mind.

The few stories he told about Washington often placed the president in some embarrassment, as when at Washington's first open house the secretary announced Washington's entrance as if he had been an emperor. Those about John Adams, likewise few in number, seem more bemused than amused. He reports Adams saying, "A boy of 15 who is not a democrat is good for nothing, and he is no better who is a democrat at 20." He reports Franklin as having said that Adams, is "always an honest man, often a great one— but sometimes absolutely mad."

The latter quotation offers a chance to see Jefferson commonplacing a quotation. What Franklin had said was that Adams was "always an honest man, often a wise one, but sometimes, and in some things, absolutely out of his senses."[13] But tracking Jefferson's sources would be a study all its own. For now, both his stories and sayings sound enough like Franklin's as to be mistaken for them, and vice versa.

In the summer of 1775 Philadelphia's *Evening Post* printed an epitaph alleged to have been copied from the grave of John Bradshaw in Jamaica, where the corpse was secreted from vengeful Royalists after the English Revolution, for Bradshaw had chaired the commission ordering Charles First to be beheaded. Jefferson adopted the epitaph as a motto, "Rebellion to Tyrants is Obedience to God,"[14] undoubtedly aware it had been concocted in committee by Franklin as a possible national motto. Typical of Jefferson, commonplacing became camouflage.

Although preferring absurdity to mere wordplay from the start, his writings show a growing concern for developing an American English language, making new words to fit a new world. He regretted that his country could not then afford a class of literati with the leisure to experiment and emulate Shakespeare's "free and magical creation of words."[15] Until that time, he urged patience:

"Certainly so great growing a population, spread over such an extent of country, with such a variety of climates, of productions, of arts, must enlarge their language, to make it answer its purpose of expressing all ideas new as well as old."

In his own practice, he showed the range available even as leisure remained subsidiary to survival. "The smooth temper and smooth style" that he recommended to young writers may be seen especially in the aphoristic words of wisdom interwoven in both private and public documents. He used plain talk in arguing for religious toleration: "It does me no injury for my neighbour to say there are twenty gods, or no god. It neither picks my pocket nor breaks my leg." He showed equal art in applying literary allusions: "Shall I become a Don

Quixote, to bring all men by force of argument to one opinion?"

Jefferson's retirement from public life gave him the leisure he wished for his country. His correspondence with old friends John Adams and James Madison show that his retirement was one of physical removal from Washington rather than of intellectual activity or even political life, as he reacted to publications by others recounting events in which he had played so intimate a part. His autobiographical writings, largely unpublished until after his death, show a fierce attempt to set the record straight for posterity. If they show relatively little wit or humor of his own, one would like to think that he left it to be uncovered by posterity too.

NOTES TO JEFFERSON INTRODUCTION

1. *Writings of Thomas Jefferson,* ed. Paul Leicester Ford, (New York: Putnam, 1892), 10:218n.

2. *Family Letters of Thomas Jefferson,* eds. E.E. Betts and J.A. Bear (Columbia: University of Missouri Press, 1966), 394–5.

3. *Diary & Autobiography,* (Cambridge: Harvard University Press, 1961) 3:335.

4. *Thomas Jefferson, Writings,* ed. Merrill D. Peterson (New York: Library of America, 1984), 707.

5. *Family Letters,* 369.

6. Ibid., 368.

7. *Writings,* 11:423–24.

8. *Journal,* ed. E.S. Maclay (New York: D. Appleton, 1890) 272.

9. *Family Letters,* 37–38.

10. Ibid., 40.

11. *Papers of Thomas Jefferson,* ed. Julian Boyd (Princeton: Princeton University Press, 1950) 15:351.

12. *Writings,* ed. Paul Leicester Ford, 10:70–71.

13. *Papers,* ed. Julian Boyd, 15:316.

14. Ibid., 1:677.

15. *Writings of Thomas Jefferson,* ed. Andrew A. Lipscomb and Albert Ellery Bergh (Washington DC: Thomas Jefferson Memorial Association, 1903–04) 13:346; 14:464.

{ 1764 }

1. St. Paul only says that it is better to be married than to burn. Now I presume that if that apostle had known that providence would at an after day be so kind to any particular set of people as to furnish them with other means of extinguishing their fire than those of matrimony, he would have earnestly recommended them to their practice.

—Responding to his friend William Fleming's jocular advice to marry. (20 March)

{ 1785 }

1. An honest heart being the first blessing, a knowing head is the second.

—Advising his nephew Peter Carr in a fatherly letter. (19 August)

2. Falsehood of the tongue leads to that of the heart.

—Ibid.

{ 1786 }

1. I will wish you a good night,—I beg your pardon. I had forgot you would have it without my wishes.

—Congratulating William Smith on marrying John Adams's daughter. (9 July)

{ 1787 }

1. Mr. Jefferson has the honour to present to Mrs. Smith and to send her the two pair of Corsets she desired. He wishes they may be suitable, as Mrs. Smith omitted to send her measure. . . . Should they be too small however, she will be so good as to lay them by a while. There are ebbs as well as flows in this world. When the mountain refused to come to Mahomet, he went to the mountain.

—Responding to John Adams's daughter, who requested he run an errand for her in Paris. (15 January)

2. Were it left to me to decide whether we should have a government without newspapers, or newspapers without a government, I should not hesitate a moment to prefer the latter.

—In a letter to friend Edward Carrington. (16 January)

3. He is less remote from the truth who believes nothing, than he who believes what is wrong.

—In *Notes on the State of Virginia*, Query 6.

4. The time to guard against corruption and tyranny is before they shall have gotten hold on us.

—Ibid., Query 13.

5. It is better to keep the wolf out of the fold, than to trust to drawing his teeth and talons after he shall have entered.

—Ibid., Query 13.

6. It does me no injury for my neighbour to say there are twenty gods, or no god. It neither picks my pocket nor breaks my leg.

—Ibid., Query 17.

7. What has been the effect of coercion? To make one half the world fools, and the other half hypocrites.

—Ibid., Query 17.

8. It is error alone which needs the support of government. Truth can stand by itself.

—Ibid., Query 17.

9. The way to silence religious disputes, is to take no notice of them.

—Ibid., Query 17.

10. Indeed, I tremble for my country when I reflect that God is just.

—Ibid., Query 18.

11. The idea of its being a new discovery was laughed at by the Philadelphians, who in their Sunday parties across the Delaware had seen every farmer's cart mounted on such wheels. The writer in the paper supposes the English workman got his idea from Homer.

But it is more likely that the Jersey farmer got the idea from thence, because ours are the only farmers who can read Homer.

—In a report to St. John de Crévecoeur from Paris describing how wagon wheels are made from a single piece of wood. (15 January)

12. I had a letter lately dated at St. Petersburg. He had but two shirts, and yet more shirts than shillings. Still he was determined to obtain the palm of being the first circumambulator of the earth. He says that having no money they kick him from place to place and thus he expects to be kicked round the globe.

—In a letter to John Banister, Jr., telling about eccentric John Ledyard, who was determined to walk across the whole world. (19 June)

{ 1788 }

1. The learned say it is a new creation; and I believe them; not for their reasons, but because it is made on an improved plan. Europe is a first idea, a crude production, before the maker knew his trade, or had made up his mind as to what he wanted.

—In a letter to Angelica Church on America's charms. (19 February)

{ 1789 }

1. A man's moral sense must be unusually strong, if slavery does not make him a thief.

were to pay their court were assembled, the President set out, preceded by Humphreys. After passing through the antechamber, the door of the inner room was thrown in and Humphreys entered first, calling out with a loud voice, "The President of the United States." The President was so much disconcerted with it that he did not recover from it the whole time of the levee, and when the company was gone he said to Humphreys, "Well, you have taken me in once, but by God you shall never take me in a second time."

—Journal entry recording an anecdote from Edmund Randolph, who had heard the story from Washington's secretary, Tobias Lear. (16 February)

2. The first public ball which took place after the President's arrival, Colonel Humphreys, Colonel W.S. Smith, and Mrs. Knox were to arrange the ceremonials. These arrangements were as follows. A sopha at the head of the room raised on several steps whereon the President and Mrs. Washington were to be seated. The gentlemen were to dance in swords. Each one when going to dance was to lead his partner to the foot of the Sopha, make a low obeisance to the President and his lady, then go and dance, and when done bring his partner again to the foot of the Sopha for new obeisances and then to retire to their chairs. It was to be understood too that gentlemen should be dressed in bags. Mrs. Knox contrived to come with the President and to follow him and Mrs. Washington to their destination, and she had the design of forcing an invitation from the

President to a seat on the Sopha. She mounted up the steps after them, unbidden, but unfortunately the wicked Sopha was so short, that when the President and Mrs. Washington were seated, there was not room for a third person; she was obliged therefore to descend in the face of the company and to sit where she could.

—A journal entry about Washington's inner circle. (10 June)

{ 1797 }

1. I do not recollect in all the animal kingdom a single species but man which is eternally and systematically employed in the destruction of its own species.

—In a letter to James Madison. (1 January)

2. The second office of this government is honorable and easy, the first is but a splendid misery.

—Explaining to Elbridge Gerry his office as vice president. (13 May)

3. Political dissension is doubtless a less evil than the lethargy of despotism, but still it is a great evil.

—Discussing party politics with Thomas Pinckney. (29 May)

{ 1799 }

1. In a conversation with Dr. Ewing, who told the President one of his sons was an aristocrat the other a Democrat. The President asked if it was not the youngest who was the Democrat. "Yes," said Ewing. "Well," said the President, "a boy of 15 who is not a de-

mocrat is good for nothing, and he is no better who is
a democrat at 20."

—A journal entry recording a bon mot by John
Adams. (January)

2. "A man from New England called one time on
George Washington when President and, going up
stairs, he met Mrs. Washington. The man asked her: 'Is
His Majesty at home?' 'Sir, Is His Majesty at Home!
Mr. Washington is at home, Sir!' "

—From the journal of a young English visitor,
Joshua Brookes, quoting Jefferson at a dinner. (10
August)

{ 1800 }

1. I have sworn upon the altar of god, eternal
hostility against every form of tyranny over the mind
of man.

—In a letter to Benjamin Rush. (23 September)

{ 1801 }

1. We are all republicans, we are all federalists.

—In his first inaugural address. (4 March)

2. No more good must be attempted than the nation can bear.

—In letter to Walter Jones. (31 March)

{ 1802 }

1. A number of English, and some French Ladies
with their husbands were assembled at Dr. Franklin's,

who spoke wretched French. Dorcas whose proficiency was not much greater, undertook on several points to set him to rights, and had become very ridiculous by some of her corrections. At that moment Temple Franklin [Franklin's grandson] entered, and in one of his freaks of assurance kissed the Lady who stood nearest to the door, and then went round the room saluting each of them; and last of all he kissed Mrs. Jay. Mrs. Jay unused to such gallantry blushed so deeply that Dr. Franklin observing it, asked why she blushed. Mrs. M immediately answered, *"Parc'qu'il a lui baissé la derriere,"* instead of *"la derniere."*

—In a letter from Benjamin Latrobe to his wife reporting an anecdote the President told about Dorcas Montgomery, a Philadelphia matron, on a visit to Paris. (30 November)

{ 1803 }

1. Peace is our passion.
—To Sir John Sinclair. (30 June)

{ 1804 }

1. Mr. Jefferson tells large stories. At table he told us that when he was at Mareseilles he saw there a Mr. Bergasse, a famous manufacturer of wines, who told him that he would make him any sort of wine he would name, and in any quantities, at six or eight sols the bottle. And though there should not be a drop of the genuine wine required in his composition, yet it should

so perfectly imitate the taste, that the most refined connoisseur should not be able to tell which was which. You never can be an hour in this man's company without something of the marvellous, like these stories.

—John Quincy Adams's diary describing the President at dinner. (23 November)

{ 1807 }

1. More blest is that nation whose silent course of happiness furnishes nothing for history to say.

—In a letter to LeComte Diodati. (29 March)

2. The man who never looks into a newspaper is better informed than he who reads them.

—In a letter to publisher John Norvell. (14 June)

3. He who knows nothing is nearer to truth than he whose mind is filled with falsehoods and errors.

—Ibid.

4. Perhaps an editor might begin a reformation in some such way as this. Divide his paper into four chapters, heading the first, Truths; second, Probabilities; third, Possibilities; fourth Lies. . . . Such an editor, too, would have to set his face against the demoralising practice of feeding the public mind habitually on slander, and the depravity of taste which this nauseous amusement induces. Defamation is becoming a necessary of life; insomuch, that a dish of tea in the morning or evening cannot be digested without this stimulant.

—Ibid.

5. There is a snail-paced gait for the advance of new ideas on the general mind.

—In a letter to Joel Barlow. (10 December)

{ 1808 }

1. Were we to act but in cases where no contrary opinion of a lawyer can be had, we should never act.

—In a letter to Albert Gallatin. (20 September)

2. When the Minister from Denmark arrived here, he waited on the President—after conversing some time Mr. Jefferson was surprised that his visitor did not take his leave—at length every topic of conversation being exhausted both sat silent—yet the minister did not go— at last dinner was evidently approaching—the Minister then rose, rubbed his forehead, looked much distressed, made his bow and retired—he immediately went to another foreign minister and told him he feared he had made some strange mistake, for he had been three hours with the President waiting for him to order him to retire—The Minister laughed and told him that the President of the United States did not order those who visited him to retire but stayed with them till they thought proper to go themselves.

—In the diary of Gallatin's 19-year-old niece Frances Few, who was visiting Jefferson. (11 October)

3. To buy off one lie is to give a premium for the invention of others.

—In a letter to William Burwell, an attempt to counter a rumor. (22 November)

4. It was one of the rules which, above all others, made Doctor Franklin the most amiable of men in society, "never to contradict anybody." If he was urged to announce an opinion, he did it rather by asking questions, as if for information, or by suggesting doubts. When I hear another express an opinion which is not mine, I say to myself, he has a right to his opinion, as I to mine; why should I question it? His error does me no injury, and shall I become a Don Quixote, to bring all men by force of argument to one opinion?

—In a letter of advice to grandson Jefferson Randolph. (24 November)

{ 1809 }

1. Mr. Smith told him the ladies *would* follow him. "That is right," said he, "since I am too old to follow them."

—In a letter, Margaret Bayard Smith quoting a conversation between her husband and the retiring President. (March)

2. "I remember in France when his friends were taking leave of Dr. Franklin, the ladies smothered him with embraces and on his introducing me [Jefferson] to them as his successor, I told him I wished he would transfer these privileges to me, but he answered, 'You are too young a man.' "

—Ibid.

{ 1810 }

1. Now men are born scholars, lawyers, doctors; in our day this was confined to poets.

—In a letter to Judge John Tyler on the low state of legal education. (26 May)

{ 1811 }

1. Nothing betrays imbecility so much as the being insensible of it.

—In a letter to Benjamin Rush. (17 August)

{ 1812 }

1. He who knows most, knows best how little he knows.

—In a legal paper on public access to beaches. (15 February)

{ 1813 }

1. Resort is had to ridicule only when reason is against us.

—In a letter to President James Madison on critics complaining about defense measures against British. (21 May)

2. The earth belongs to the living, not to the dead.

—Writing to his son-in-law John Wayles Eppes, on the national debt. (24 June)

3. No one has a natural right to the trade of a money lender, but he who has the money to lend.

—Ibid.

{ 1814 }

1. Merchants have no country.
—In a letter, to geographer H.G. Spafford. (17 March)

2. The hour of emancipation is advancing in the march of time.
—In acknowledging a letter on slavery by young Edward Coles. (25 August)

{ 1815 }

1. Nothing is more incumbent on the old, than to know when they should get out of the way.
—In a letter to John Vaughan. (5 February)

{ 1816 }

1. If a nation expects to be ignorant and free, in a state of civilization, it expects what never was and never will be.
—In a letter to Charles Yancey on state and national politics. (6 January)

2. Where the press is free, and every man able to read, all is safe.
—Ibid.

3. You love them as infants whom you are afraid to trust without nurses; and I as adults whom I freely leave to self-government.
—Responding to physiocrat P.S. Dupont's proposal for a constitution for South American countries,

which would not give workers full civil rights. (24 April)

4. No man has a natural right to commit aggression on the equal rights of another; and this is all from which the laws ought to restrain him.

—In a letter to Francis W. Gilmer. (7 June)

5. The man who fears no truths has nothing to fear from lies.

—In letter to George Logan. (20 June)

6. Forty years of experience in government is worth a century of book-reading.

—In a letter to Samuel Kercheval. (12 July)

7. Laws and institutions must go hand in hand with the progress of the human mind.

—Ibid.

8. It is in our lives, and not from our words, that our religion must be read.

—In a letter to Margaret Bayard Smith. (6 August)

9. There would never have been an infidel, if there had never been a priest.

—Ibid.

10. Virtue and interest are inseparable.

—In a letter to George Logan. (12 November)

{ 1817 }

1. Our next meeting must then be in the country to which they have flown—a country for us not now very distant. For this journey we shall need neither gold nor silver in our purse, nor scrip, nor coats, nor staves. Nor is the provision for it more easy than the preparation has

been kind. Nothing proves more than this, that the Being who presides over the world is essentially benevolent. Stealing from us, one by one, the faculties of enjoyment, searing our sensibilities, leading us, like the horse in his mill, round and round the same beaten circle . . . until satiated and fatigued with this leaden iteration, we ask our congé. I heard once a very old friend, who had troubled himself with neither poets, nor philosophers, say the same thing in plain prose, that he was tired of pulling off his shoes and stockings at night, and putting them on again in the morning.

　　—A nostalgic review of passing years in a letter to Abigail Adams. (11 January)

　　2. No national crime passes unpunished in the long run.

　　—In a letter to François de Marbois ruminating on the excesses of the French Revolution. (14 June)

　　3. My theory has always been, that if we are to dream, the flatteries of hope are as cheap, and pleasanter than the gloom of despair.

　　—Ibid.

　　4. 1. Never spend your money before you have it.

　　　2. Never buy what you don't want, because it is cheap: it will be dear to you.

　　　3. Pride costs more than hunger, thirst and cold.

　　　4. Never put off till tomorrow what you can do today.

5. Never trouble another for what you can do yourself.

6. Think as you please and let others do so: you will then have no disputes.

7. How much pains have cost us the things which have never happened.

8. Take things always by their smooth handle.

9. When angry count 10 before you speak. If very angry 100.

10. When at table, remember that we never repent of having eaten or drunk too little.

—Sending a "little bundle of canons of conduct" for Paul Aurelius Clay, son of his old friend, Rev. Charles Clay. (12 July)

5. You can easily correct this bill to the taste of my brother lawyers, by making every other word a "said" or "aforesaid," and saying everything over two or three times, so that nobody but we of the craft can untwist the diction, and find out what it means; and that, too, not so plainly but that we may conscientiously divide one half on each side.

—In a letter to Joseph C. Cabell, enclosing a draft of a bill to set up public schools. (9 September)

{ 1818 }

1. "When I was in London, in such a year, there was a weekly club of Physicians, of which Sir John

Pringle was President, and I was invited by my friend Dr. Fothergill to attend when convenient. Their rule was to propose a thesis one week, and discuss it the next. I happened there when the question to be considered was whether Physicians had, on the whole, done most good or harm? The young members, particularly, having discussed it very learnedly and eloquently till the subject was exhausted, one of them observed to Sir John Pringle, that, altho' it was not usual for the President to take part in a debate, yet they were desirous to know his opinion on the question. He said, they must first tell him whether, under the appellation of Physicians, they meant to include old women; if they did, he thought they had done more good than harm, otherwise more harm than good."

—In a letter to Robert Walsh, who sought help in writing a sketch of Franklin's life for *Delaplaine's Repository,* quoting Franklin's story about the value of medicine. (4 December)

2. The confederation of the States, while on the carpet before the old Congress, was strenuously opposed by the smaller states, under apprehensions that they would be swallowed up by the larger ones. We were long engaged in the discussion; it produced great heats, much ill humor, and intemperate declarations from some members. Dr. Franklin at length brought the debate to a close with one of his little apologues. He observed that "at the time of the Union of England and Scotland, the Duke of Argyle was most violently op-

posed to that measure, and among other things predicted that, as the whale had swallowed Jonas, so Scotland would be swallowed by England. However," said the Doctor, "when Lord Bute came into the government, he soon brought into it's administration so many of his countrymen that it was found in event that Jonas swallowed the whale." This little story produced a general laugh, restored good humor, and the Article of difficulty passed.

—Ibid.

3. When Dr. Franklin went to France on his revolutionary mission, his eminence as a philosopher, his venerable appearance, and the cause on which he was sent, rendered him extremely popular. For all ranks and conditions of men there, entered warmly into the American interest. He was therefore feasted and invited to all the court parties. At these he sometimes met the old Duchess of Bourbon, who being a chess player of about his force, they very generally played together. Happening once to put her king into prise, the Doctor took it. "Ah," says she, "we do not take kings so." "We do in America," said the Doctor.

—Ibid.

4. At one of these parties, the emperor Joseph II, then at Paris, incognito under the title of Count Falkenstein, was overlooking the game, in silence, while the company was engaged in animated conversations on the American question. "How happens it M. le Comte," said the Duchess, "that while we all feel so much inter-

est in the cause of the Americans, you say nothing for them?" "I am a king by trade," said he.

—Ibid.

5. When the Declaration of Independence was under the consideration of Congress, there were two or three unlucky expressions in it which gave offence to some members. The words "Scotch and other foreign auxiliaries" excited the ire of a gentleman or two of that country. Severe strictures on the conduct of the British king, in negativing our repeated repeals of the law which permitted the importation of slaves, were disapproved by some Southern gentlemen whose reflections were not yet matured to the full abhorrence of that traffic. Altho' the offensive expressions were immediately yielded, these gentlemen continued their depredations on other parts of the instrument. I was sitting by Dr. Franklin who perceived that I was not insensible to these mutilations. "I have made it a rule," said he, "whenever in my power, to avoid becoming the draughtsman of papers to be reviewed by a public body. I took my lesson from an incident which I will relate to you. When I was a journeyman printer, one of my companions, an apprentice Hatter, having served out his time, was about to open shop for himself, his first concern was to have a handsome signboard, with a proper inscription. He composed it in these words "John Thompson, *Hatter, makes and sells hats for ready money,*" with a figure of a hat subjoined. But he thought he would submit it to his friends for their amendments.

The first he shewed it to thought the word "Hatter" tautologous, because followed by the words "makes hats" which shew he was a Hatter. It was struck out. The next observed that the word "makes" might as well be omitted, because his customers would not care who made the hats. If good and to their mind, they would buy by whomsoever made. He struck it out. A third said he thought the words *"for ready money,"* were useless as it was not the custom of the place to sell on credit. Every one who purchased expected to pay. They were parted with, and the inscription now stood "John Thompson sells hats." *"Sells hats!"* says his next friend. "Why, nobody will expect you to give them away. What then is the use of that word?" It was stricken out, and *"hats"* followed it,— the rather as there was one painted on the board. So his inscription was reduced ultimately to "John Thompson" with the figure of a hat subjoined.

—Ibid.

6. He had a party to dine with him one day at Passy of whom one half were Americans, the other half French and among the last was the Abbé [Raynal]. During the dinner he got on his favorite theory of the degeneracy of animals and even of man, in America, and urged it with his usual eloquence. The Doctor at length noticing the accidental stature and positions of his guests, at table, "Come," says he, "M. L'Abbé, let us try this question by the fact before us. We are here one half Americans, and one half French, and it happens that the Americans have placed themselves on one side of the

table, and our French friends are on the other. Let both parties rise and we will see on which side nature has degenerated." It happened that his American guests were Carmichael, Harmer, Humphreys and others of the finest stature and form, while those of the other side were remarkably diminutive, and the Abbé himself particularly was a mere shrimp. He parried the appeal however, by a complimentary admission of exceptions, among which the Doctor himself was a conspicuous one.

—Ibid.

7. The Doctor and Silas Deane were in conversation one day at Passy on the numerous errors in the Abbé's *Histoire des deux Indes*, when he happened to step in. After the usual salutations, Silas Deane said to him "The Doctor and myself Abbé, were just speaking of the errors of fact into which you have been led in your history." "Oh no, Sir," said the Abbé, "that is impossible. I took the greatest care not to insert a single fact, for which I had not the most unquestionable authority." "Why," says Deane, "there is the story of Polly Baker, and the eloquent apology you have put into her mouth, when brought before a court of Massachusetts to suffer punishment under a law, which you cite, for having had a bastard. I know there never was such a law in Massachusetts." "Be assured," said the Abbé, "you are mistaken, and that that is a true story. I do not immediately recollect indeed the particular information on

which I quote it, but I am certain that I had for it unquestionable authority." Doctor Franklin who had been for some time shaking with restrained laughter at the Abbé's confidence in his authority for the tale, said, "I will tell you, Abbé, the origin of that story. When I was a printer and editor of a newspaper, we were sometimes slack of news, and to amuse our customers, I used to fill up our vacant columns with anecdotes, and fables, and fancies of my own, and this of Polly Baker is a story of my making, on one of those occasions." The Abbé without the least disconcert, exclaimed with a laugh, "Oh, very well, Doctor, I had rather relate your stories than other men's truths."

—Ibid.

{ 1820 }

1. Men in glass houses should not provoke a war of stones.

—In a letter to Robert Walsh complimenting him on his reply to British libels of Americans. (6 February)

2. This momentous question, like a fire bell in the night, awakened and filled me with terror. I considered it at once as the knell of the Union.

—In a letter to John Holmes regarding the Missouri Compromise on slave vs. free states. (22 April)

3. Our right may be doubted of mortgaging posterity for the expences of a war in which they will have a right to say their interests were not concerned. It is in-

cumbent on every generation to pay its own debt as it goes. A principle, which, if acted on, would save one half the wars of the world.

—In a letter to Destutt de Tracy, on justifying neutrality in a European war. (26 December)

{ 1821 }

1. That one hundred and fifty lawyers should do business together ought not to be expected.

—In his autobiography, commenting on Congress. (6 January)

2. He mentioned the Eddystone lighthouse in the British Channel as being built on a rock in the mid-channel, totally inaccessible in winter, from the boisterous character of that sea, in that season. That therefore, for the two keepers employed to keep up the lights, all provisions for the winter were necessarily carried to them in autumn, as they could never be visited again till the return of the milder season. That on the first practicable day in the spring a boat put off to them with fresh supplies. The boatmen met at the door one of the keepers and accosted him with a "How goes it friend?" "Very well." "How is your companion?" "I do not know." "Don't know? Is not he here?" "I can't tell." "Have not you seen him today?" "No." "When did you see him?" "Not since last fall." "You have killed him?" "Not I, indeed." They were about to lay hold of him, as having certainly murdered his companion; but he desired them to go up stairs and examine for themselves.

They went up, and there found the other keeper. They had quarrelled it seems soon after being left there, and divided into two parties, assigned the cares below to one, and those above to the other, and had never spoken to or seen one another since.

—Ibid., recalling Franklin as he talked about "the singular disposition of men to quarrel and divide into parties."

{ 1822 }

1. The life of the feeder is better than that of the fighter.

—In a letter to John Adams commenting on wars in Europe. (1 June)

{ 1823 }

1. The generation which commences a revolution rarely completes it.

—Ibid., on revolutions in South America. (4 September)

{ 1824 }

1. One evening he called about twilight and being shown into the drawing room without being announced, he found Mr. Jefferson seated on the floor, surrounded by half a dozen of his little grandchildren so eagerly and noisily engaged in a game of romps that for some moments his entrance was not perceived. When his presence was discovered Mr. Jefferson rose up and shak-

ing hands with him, said, "You have found me playing the fool, Baron, but I am sure to *you* I need make no apology."

—A visit from Baron von Humboldt recorded in the notebook of Margaret Bayard Smith.

{ 1826 }

1. The general spread of the light of science has already laid open to every view the palpable truth, that the mass of mankind has not been born with saddles on their backs, nor a favored few booted and spurred, ready to ride them legitimately, by the grace of God.

—To Roger C. Weightman turning down an invitation to the official celebration of Independence. (24 June)

{ 1834 }

1. Mr. Jefferson with a smile remarked, "that he had heard of a University somewhere, in which the Professorship of Mathematics was hereditary."

—An anecdote from James Madison about Jefferson's replying to those who wished hereditary offices in B.L. Rayner's *Life of Thomas Jefferson.*

2. A gentleman from Baltimore, an invited guest, who accidentally sat next to him, asked permission to wish him joy. "I would advise you," answered Jefferson, smiling, "to follow my example on nuptial occasions,

when I always tell the bridegroom I will wait till the end of the year before offering my congratulations."

—Ibid., Rayner describing dinner following the inauguration.

{ 1837 }

1. The house at Shadwell, in which he lived with his mother, caught fire, while they were on a visit to a neighbour; and in the alarm and confusion of the slaves, almost everything in it was consumed. The one who brought him the first tidings of his misfortune, knowing his master's passion for music, in which he probably participated, thus unconsciously parodied Francis the First's consolation to his mother after the battle of Pavia [i.e., All is lost save honor.]— "But, master, we have saved the fiddle."

—In George Tucker's authoritative biography, *The Life of Thomas Jefferson*, 2 vols. (London: Charles Knight, 1837) 1:44, telling of the fire that destroyed the home at Shadwell in 1770.

{ 1841 }

1. In the course of the evening, someone remarked to him, "You look so happy and satisfied Mr. Jefferson, and Mr. Madison looks so serious not to say sad, that a spectator might imagine that you were the one coming in, and he the one going out of office." "There's good reason for my happy and his serious looks," replied Mr.

Jefferson, "I have got the burthen off my shoulders, while he has now got it on his."

—Margaret Bayard Smith recollecting Jefferson at Madison's inaugural ball. (c. 1841)

{ 1858 }

1. He never indulged in controversial conversation, because it often excited unpleasant feeling, and illustrated its inutility by the anecdote of two men who sat down candidly to discuss a subject and each converted the other.

—In Henry S. Randall's reliable biography, grandson Thomas Jefferson Randolph recalling his grandfather.

2. "It is not," Jefferson was wont to observe, "to physic that I object so much as to physicians." Occasionally, too, he would speak jocularly, especially to the unprofessional, of medical practice . . . that whenever he saw three physicians together he looked up to discover whether there was not a turkey buzzard in the neighborhood.

—Ibid., Randall quoting a physician who visited Jefferson's home.

3. On riding out with him, when a lad, we met a negro who bowed to us. He returned his bow, I did not. Turning to me, he asked, "Do you permit a negro to be more of a gentleman than yourself?"

—Ibid., Randolph recalling a lesson of Jefferson's concerning manners.

4. He exemplified it by an incident which occurred to a young gentleman returned from Europe, where he had been educated. On riding out with his companions, the strap of his girth broke at the hole of the buckle; and they, perceiving it an accident easily remedied, rode on and left him. A plain man coming up and seeing that his horse made a circular path in the road in his impatience to get on, asked if he could aid him? "Oh, sir," replied the young man, "if you could only assist me to get it up to the next hole." "Suppose you let it out a hole or two on the other side," said the man.

—Ibid., Randolph recalling his grandfather's low estimate of education that ignored practical life.

{ 1871 }

1. Jefferson remarked to his friend that, though the ways of Divine Providence were all wise and beneficent, yet it had always struck him as being strange that the thick, fleshly coverings and defenses of the bones in the limbs of the human frame were placed in their rear, when the danger of their fracture generally came from the front. . . . "Well," cried Dr. Stuart, raising his hands in horror, "What is the world coming to! Here this fellow Jefferson, after turning upside down everything on earth, is now quarreling with God Almighty himself!"

—Jefferson's reflection upon nursing a slave's injured leg, as told in great-granddaughter Sarah N. Randolph's memoir.

2. "It is hard to tell, because he always took the right side."

—Ibid., the reply of old-time neighbor asked to judge Jefferson's skill in arguing a case.

3. While the question of Independence was before Congress, it had its meetings near a livery-stable. The members wore short breeches and silk stockings, and, with handkerchief in hand, they were diligently employed in lashing the flies from their legs. So very vexatious was this annoyance, and to so great an impatience did it arouse the sufferers, that it hastened, if it did not aid, in inducing them to promptly affix their signatures to the great document which gave birth to an entire republic.

—Ibid., Randolph recollecting one of Jefferson's anecdotes, probably unaware that he was telling what Adams called one of his "large stories."

APPENDIX:

SOURCES AND RESOURCES

ᘒᔑᕽᘒ

U NLESS OTHERWISE identified, the excerpts in the Franklin and Washington sections are from my scholarly editions: *Ben Franklin Laughing* (Berkeley: University of California Press, 1980) and *George Washington Laughing* (New Haven: Archon Books, 1989). Entries from Franklin's publications are from first editions; those from Washington's correspondence are from his papers at the Huntington or the Library of Congress. Inquiring readers may collate these and the other excerpts conveniently in the series of volumes being issued as the Library of America: *Benjamin Franklin, Writings,* ed. J.A. Leo Lemay (New York: Library of America, 1987), *George Washington, Writings,* ed. John Rhodehamel (scheduled for 1997), and *Thomas Jefferson, Writings,* ed. Merrill Peterson (New York: Library of America, 1984).

Exhaustive scholarly editions have been appearing from these university presses over the past half-century: *The Papers of Benjamin Franklin,* ed. Leonard Labarree, et al. (New Haven: Yale University Press, 1959–   ); *The Papers of George Washington,* ed. W.W. Abott and Dorothy Twohig (Charlottesville: University Press of Virginia, 1983–   ); *Diaries of*

{ 163 }

George Washington, ed. Donald Jackson (Charlottesville: University Press of Virginia, 1976–1979); *Diary and Autobiography of John Adams,* ed. Lyman H. Butterfield, et al. (Cambridge: Belknap Press of Harvard University, 1961); and *The Papers of Thomas Jefferson,* ed. Julian Boyd (Princeton: Princeton University Press, 1950–   ). In the following lists, these are abbreviated respectively as PF, PW, PA and DA, and PJ.

Unless otherwise identified: My Adams entries derive from the older edition, *The Works of John Adams,* ed. Charles Francis Adams (Boston: Little, Brown, 1850) abbreviated CFA; along with *The Adams-Jefferson Letters,* ed. Lester J. Capon (Chapel Hill: University of North Carolina Press, 1959) abbreviated A-JL. The Jefferson entries derive from Paul Leicester Ford's edition, *The Writings of Thomas Jefferson* (New York: G.P. Putnam, 1899) abbreviated *Ford;* or *The Writings of Thomas Jefferson,* ed. Henry A. Washington (Washington DC: U.S. Congress, 1854) abbreviated HAW; or *The Family Letters of Thomas Jefferson,* ed. Edwin M. Betts and James A. Bear, Jr. (Columbia: University of Missouri Press, 1966) abbreviated B&B.

References in each section are listed separately by year and entry under that year; e.g., 1728.1 means the first entry under the year 1728. When the references are to multiple entries, they are listed merely under the pertinent years; e.g. 1728–1745.6 means that *all* entries down to the sixth under year 1745 are from the same source(s), in this case *Poor Richard* almanacs, abbreviated PRA or the *Pennsylvania Gazette,* abbreviated PaG.

FRANKLIN REFERENCE LIST

1728.	Lemay, Library of America (LoA) 91
1738.1	Ibid, 426
1745.6	Ibid, 302–303
1753.2	Ibid, 471–472
1755.3	PF 6:242
1756.2	Ibid, 365
1757.2	Lemay, LoA 488
1758.6	Ibid, 532
1762.1	PF 10:147
1763.1	Ibid, 288
1765–1766.4	Lemay LoA 561–587
1768.1–2	PF 15:151–152, 66–67
1769.1	PF 16:40
1770.1	PF 17:239
1771.1	Lemay LoA 1338–39
1772.1	PF 19:46
1773.1	Lemay LoA 881
.2	PF 20:464
1775.3	Lemay LoA 692
1778.4	Ibid, 921
1779.1	PF 30:598
1780.1	Lemay LoA 1018
.3	*The Writings of Benjamin Franklin,* ed. Albert H. Smyth (New York: Macmillan, 1907), 8:189
1781.1	Ibid, 8:316
1781.2–5	*Early Life of Samuel Rogers,* ed. P.W. Clayden (London: Smith, Elder, 1887), pp. 266–268
1782.1–2	Lemay LoA 1047–48
1783.1	Ibid, 1073
1784.1–4	Ibid, 1085–89
1784.5	*Writings,* ed. Smyth, 9:224
1784.6–7	Lemay LoA 1100, 977

1784.8   *Writings,* ed. Smyth, 9:237

1784.9   Lemay LoA 1096

1785.1   *Writings,* ed. Smyth, 9:329

1785.2   Lemay LoA 1107

1786.2   Ibid, 1390

1787.2–3 Ibid, 1139–40

1789.1   *Writings,* ed. Smyth, 10:69

1790.2   *Letters of Benjamin Rush,* ed. Lyman H.
          Butterfield (Princeton: Princeton University Press,
          1951), 1:564

For all other Franklin references see *Ben Franklin Laughing,* ed. P.M. Zall (Berkeley: University of California Press, 1980).

WASHINGTON REFERENCE LIST

Unless otherwise indicated, all entries are from *George Washington Laughing,* ed. P.M. Zall (New Haven: Archon Books, 1989). The exceptions are:

1760.1–2 *Writings of Washington,* ed. John C. Fitzpatrick
          (Washington DC: Government Printing Office,
          1932–40), 1:111, 112.

1797.2   *Worthy Partner: the Papers of Martha Washington,*
          ed. Joseph E. Fields (Westport CT: Greenwood,
          1994), 464.

ADAMS REFERENCE LIST

1759.1   *Diary and Autobiography,* ed. Lyman H. Butterfield
          (Cambridge: Belknap Press of Harvard University,
          1961), 1:95. Hereafter DA.

1759.2   Ibid, 1:101

1759.3	Ibid, 1:77
1759.4	Ibid, 1:120
1760.1–2	Ibid, 171–172
1762.1	Ibid, 1:232
1763.1–3	*Papers of John Adams,* ed. R. J. Taylor, et al. (Cambridge: Belknap Press of Harvard University, 1977–89), 1:92–93.
1771.1–3	DA 2:8–9
1771.4	Ibid, 2:14
1771.5	Ibid, 2:31
1772.1	Ibid, 2:65
1774.1	Ibid, 2:132
1775.1	*Book of Abigail & John,* ed. Lyman H. Butterfield, et al. (Cambridge: Harvard University Press, 1975), 109–110.
1776.1	DA 3:418
1778.1	Ibid, 2:290–91
1778.2–5	Ibid, 4:36–37, 78–79, 79, 80–81
1778.6	Ibid, 2:309
1778.7	Ibid, 2:314
1778.8	*Works of John Adams,* ed. Charles Francis Adams (Boston: Little, Brown, 1850), 9:476; hereafter abbreviated CFA
1782.1	DA 3:71
1783.1	CFA 1:403
1783.2	*Adams-Jefferson Letters,* ed. Lester J. Cappon (Chapel Hill: University of North Carolina Press, 1959), 1:121; hereafter A-JL.
1786.1	DA 3:193
1790.1	*Old Family Letters,* ed. Alexander Biddle (Philadelphia: J.B. Lippincott, 1892), 55–56
1797.1	Julian Niemcewicz, *Under Their Vine & Fig Tree,* ed. M.J.E. Budka (Elizabeth NJ: Grassman Publishing, 1965), 29–30.

1800.1   CFA 9:588

1812.1–2   *The Spur of Fame,* ed. Douglass Adair & John Schutz
            (San Marino CA: Huntington Library Press, 1966),
            225, 235

1813.1–2   A-JL 2:354, 399

1816.1–2   CFA 10:219, 221

1817.1   A-JL 2:509

1820.1   Ibid, 2:559

1820.2   Charles W. March, *Reminiscences of Congress*
            (New York: Baker & Scribner, 1850), 62

1820.3   Sarah Randolph, *Domestic Life of Thomas Jefferson*
            (New York: Harpers, 1871), 421n.

JEFFERSON REFERENCE LIST

1764.1   *Papers of Thomas Jefferson,* ed. Julian Boyd, et al.
            (Princeton: Princeton University Press, 1950–   ),
            1:16; hereafter abbreviated PJ.

1785.1–2   Ibid, 8:406

1786.1   *Collections of the Massachusetts Historical Society* 7 s.
            (Boston: Massachusetts Historical Society, 1900),
            1:20

1787.1–2   PJ 11:45, 49

1787.3–10   Peterson, ed. LoA, 156, 246, 285, 286, 287, 289

1787.11–12 PJ 11:44, 476–77

1788.1   Ibid, 12:601

1789.1   Ibid, 14:492

1790.1–2   Ibid, 16:129

1791.1   Ibid, 19:113

1793.1–2   *Writings of Thomas Jefferson,* ed. H.A. Washington
            (Washington DC: Congress, 1854), 9:132, 147; here-
            after HAW.

1797.1–3   *Writings of Thomas Jefferson*, ed. Paul Leicester Ford (New York: G.P. Putnam, 1892), 7:100, 120, 128; hereafter "Ford."

1799.1   Ibid 7:280

1799.2   *New York Historical Society Quarterly* 31 (1947):81–82

1800.1   Ford 7:458

1801.1   Ibid, 8:3

1801.2   HAW 4:393

1802.1   *Papers of Henry Latrobe*, ed. John VanHorne, et al. (New Haven: Yale University Press, 1984), 1:235

1803.1   HAW 4:491

1804.1   John Quincy Adams, *Memoirs*, ed. Charles Francis Adams (Philadelphia: Lippincott, 1874), 1:317

1807.1   HAW 5:62

1807.2–5   Ford 9:73, 74, 169

1808.1   HAW 5:369

1808.2   *Journal of Southern History* 29 (1963): 350–51

1808.3–4   Ford 9:229, 233

1809.1–2   Margaret Bayard Smith, *Forty Years of Washington Society,* ed. Gaillord Hunt (London: Fisher, Unwin, 1906), p. 59

1810.1   Ford 9:277n.

1811.1   Ibid, 9:328

1812.1   *Writings of Thomas Jefferson,* ed. Andrew A. Lipscomb & Albert Ellery Bergh (Washington DC: Thomas Jefferson Memorial Association, 1903–04), 18:130

1813.1–3   Ford 9:382, 389, 394

1814.1   HAW 6:334

1814.2   Ford 9:478

1815.1   HAW 6:417

1816.1–7   Ford 10:4, 23, 32, 27, 42

1816.8–9   HAW 7:28

1816.10   Ford 10:69

1817.1   Henry S. Randall, *Life of Thomas Jefferson* (New York: Derby & Jackson, 1858), 3:439–40

1817.2–3   HAW 7:76, 77

1817.4   Ford 10:93n.

1817.5   *Writings,* ed. Lipscomb & Bergh, 17:417–18

1818.1–7   Ford 10:118–21

1820.1–3   Ibid, 10:155, 157, 175

1821.1–2   Ibid, 1:82, 76

1822.1   Ibid, 10:217

1823.1   Ibid, 10:269

1824.1   Smith, *Forty Years of Washington Society,* p. 396

1826.1   Ford 10:391

1834.1–2   B.L. Rayner, *Life of Thomas Jefferson* (Boston: Lilly, Wait, Coleman & Holden, 1834), pp. 23, 304

1837.1   George Tucker, *Life of Thomas Jefferson* (London: Charles Knight, 1837), 1:44

1841.1   Smith, *Forty Years of Washington Society,* p. 412

1858.1   Randall, *Life of Thomas Jefferson,* 1:403

1858.2–4   Ibid, 3:514, 674, 675

1871.1–3   Sarah Randolph, *Domestic Life of Thomas Jefferson* (New York: Harpers, 1871), 328, 40, 49n

ABOUT THE EDITOR

Native of Lowell, Massachusetts, with degrees from Swarthmore College and Harvard University (PhD), Paul M. Zall taught for forty years at Cornell, Oregon, and Cal State Los Angeles before retiring to become a research scholar at the Huntington Library, San Marino, California. There he has published two dozen books, chiefly on British and American humor along with studies of the Founding Fathers, their wives, and their children. He has been featured on both commercial and educational television, and serves as consultant on such series as the Learning Channel's "American Revolution, with Charles Kuralt." His current research focuses on establishing an authentic version of Thomas Jefferson's autobiographical writings.